KT-480-966

CONTENTS

List of tables

FACT FILE one

FACT FILE two

FOREWORD

The latest in Euromonitor's series of economic handbooks examines the political, economic, and social structure of the European community and the other principal countries of Western Europe. This region of some 350 million inhabitants includes some of the richest and most affluent nations in the world with a highly developed industrial base, a skilled workforce, and a highly developed service sector. But the last decade has brought many problems for the European economy with its dependence on oil imports and rising levels of unemployment, while there are now real fears that Europe is falling behind in the race towards new technologies.

The handbook is presented in twelve chapters, each discussing a major current theme relevant to European economic development. Commencing with an overview which sets Western Europe with the world economy as a whole, the handbook proceeds to discuss such aspects as the role of the European Community; political structure and defence; current economic and industrial development, trade, finance and banking and the European consumer market.

The WEST EUROPEAN ECONOMIC HANDBOOK is an indispensable source of reference for up-to-date information and analysis of economic trends and developments on this leading world region. The handbook concludes with a comprehensive series of statistical tabulations featuring up-to-date socio-economic and marketing statistics.

The handbook has been compiled by Euromonitor utilising our extensive European network of economists, business writers and market analysts.

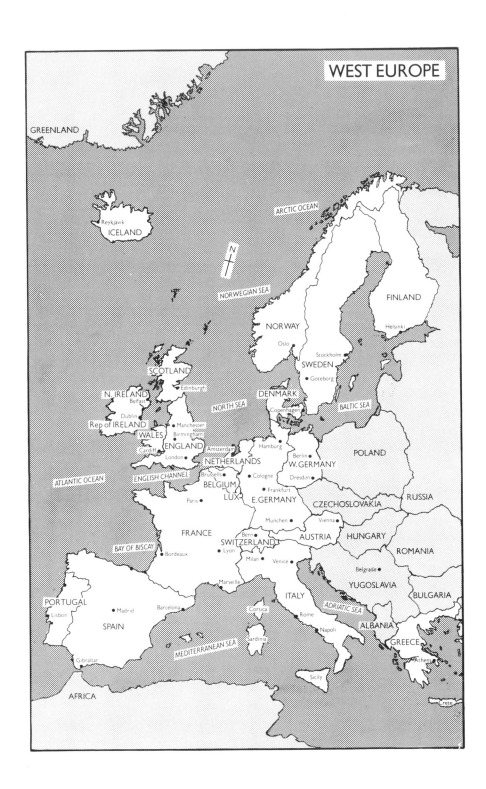

CHAPTER ONE
WESTERN EUROPE:
AN INTERNATIONAL PERSPECTIVE

I   Introduction

When the countries of Western Europe are pictured as a single group, they constitute one of the largest and richest markets of the world. The same applies in terms of the area's economic base. Although relatively poor in natural resources, the region's infrastructure, industrial capabilities and pool of skilled workers is vast. These accomplishments are reflected by West Europe's prominence in the world economy. In 1985, the region claimed less than 10 per cent of the world's population excluding China yet it accounted for more than 30 per cent of the world GDP and manufacturing value added (at constant prices). In summary, there are abundant reasons why West European consumers, producers and workers can regard their economic achievements with satisfaction and look to the future with a confidence which would be unjustified in other corners of the world.

But alongside this comforting impression of economic security is a more disconcerting set of trends. As a region, West Europe has usually looked for safety first – wars, recessions and maturity have made it that way. Europessimism has been a fashion that comes and goes and, today, it is in vogue again. Though West Europe's economies have grown only feebly in the 1980s, that experience is not a unique one. The entire world now appears to have entered a prolonged period of slow growth. The difference is that the current version of Europessimism points to problems of a more fundamental and lasting nature. Slow growth is not the only prominent feature of the modern world economy. It is also marked by a degree of technological and economic change which does not favour natural caution. The ability of West Europe's economies to adapt and thrive in this sort of economic environment is being questioned.

Many pessimists' fears involve supply-side issues. One example is the comparatively dismal performance of labour markets in West Europe. In 1973, when the first oil price shock occurred, the region's total employment was 160 million. During the next thirteen years it lost nearly 6 million jobs – all at a time when more than 20 million jobs were being created in the USA and Japan was adding another 6 million.

Another concern is that West Europe is faltering in the development and application of emerging technologies at a time when the industrialized world is in the midst of a new technological revolution. If the region is unable to follow the USA and Japan into the new science- and technology-based industries of the 1990s, its ability to generate wealth and to sustain its current standard of living will be jeopardized. A third disturbing feature is the sluggish growth of investment in West Europe coupled with the impression of some analysts that existing mechanisms for allocating capital are strikingly inefficient.

The two contrasting views on West Europe's economic health and prospects can both claim support from broad cross-sections of European society. And to some extent, both versions are accurate. Despite their shared cultures, institutions and heritage, West European countries remain quite different in many ways. Their achievements and prospects vary accordingly. Whatever the circumstances of the country or industry in question, a wealth of previous economic achievements remains available and the opportunities to redress problems in lagging fields promise to be rewarding for both European firms and societies.

The first section of this chapter looks at the region in a global context, highlighting some of the features which distinguish it from other parts of the world. A comparison of macroeconomic trends in West Europe and in other industrialized markets is carried out in the second section, followed by an overview of trading patterns, major markets and suppliers. The chapter concludes by looking at economic relations between West Europe and other regions of the world.

II The region in a global context

Figure 1 shows growth performance in Western Europe and the

**FIGURE 1.1   GROWTH PERFORMANCE OF WEST EUROPE AND THE
WORLD
(average annual growth rate for total output)**[a]

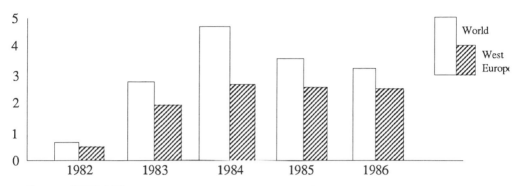

Source: ECE, UN
[a] Output is measured in terms of real GDP for all countries except those of Eastern
Europe. Net material production is the output measure used in the latter group.

world during the years 1982–86. Although world growth has
weakened since 1984, the pace of expansion in West Europe has
changed very little. The region's growth performance, however, has
consistently failed to match that of the world as a whole.

West Europe's feeble economic recovery becomes even more
apparent when considered in relation to its major economic rivals.
According to the data in Table 1.1, GDP grew at a rate of 2.5 per cent
in 1986. This was roughly the pace in the two preceding years and
somewhat greater than the figure for 1983 (1.6 per cent). Such a
performance is not impressive when measured by the experience of
the USA or Japan. Growth in 1986 matched that of the USA but in
earlier years the European recovery generally proceeded at a much
slower pace than in other industrialized areas.

The comparatively modest growth record of West Europe owes
much to the slow pace of investment. In 1985, total investment
accounted for little more than 10 per cent of the region's growth,
meaning that the upturn in economic activity lacked the momentum
attained throughout the rest of the industrialized world. The poor
investment performance is reflected in the data for gross domestic
fixed capital formation (GFCF) in Table 1.1 (see p.4). Growth rates

TABLE 1.1 GROWTH OF GDP, PRIVATE CONSUMPTION AND FIXED CAPITAL FORMATION [a]
(percentage change over previous year)

| | GDP | | | | Private consumption | | | | Gross domestic fixed capital formation | | | |
| | West Europe | Of which: | | | West Europe | Of which: | | | West Europe | Of which: | | |
		EEC	USA	Japan		EEC	USA	Japan		EEC	USA	Japan
1981	0.0	-0.2	1.9	3.7	0.0	0.1	1.2	1.3	-4.0	-4.5	1.1	3.1
1982	0.5	0.4	-1.9	3.1	0.8	0.7	1.3	4.1	-1.9	-1.8	-9.6	0.8
1983	1.6	1.6	3.6	3.2	1.4	1.4	4.6	3.2	0.6	0.3	8.2	-0.3
1984	2.5	2.3	6.4	5.1	1.3	1.2	4.7	2.8	2.0	2.0	16.1	4.6
1985	2.4	2.3	2.7	4.6	2.4	2.0	3.5	2.7	2.3	2.1	7.7	5.6
1986	2.5	—	2.5	—	3.7	—	4.0	—	4.0	—	1.6	—

Source: OECD, IMF and author's calculations
[a] Calculated at 1975 prices and exchange rates

were negative in the first years of this decade and have usually been lower than the corresponding figures for Japan and the USA. Partially because of the feeble investment performance, private consumption has provided the major impetus for Europe's recovery. But even in this field, European rates of growth have been considerably less than the figures for the USA and Japan.

Table 1.2 draws together data showing per capita figures for three components of national accounts in each of the world's major industrialized markets. In 1975, per capita GDP in West Europe exceeded that of Japan and was roughly 15 per cent less than the US figures. By the mid-1980s, Japan had overtaken West Europe while the gap with the USA remained. Estimates of MVA per capita show a more pronounced deterioration in Western Europe's relative position. The region's per capita MVA in 1975 matched that of the USA and was far larger than the Japanese figure. That situation had changed considerably by the mid-1980s: Western Europe has fallen slightly behind the USA while MVA per capita was less than three-quarters of the level in Japan.

TABLE 1.2   INTERNATIONAL ECONOMIC PERFORMANCE:
A COMPARISON OF PER CAPITA LEVELS
(in 1980 $US)

		GDP	MVA	Gross fixed capital formation
West Europe	1975	8753	2363	1936
	1984	10294	2655	2044
Japan	1975	7264	1783	2350
	1984	10222	3596	3125
USA	1975	10329	2264	1810
	1984	12420	2810	2497

Source: UN
GDP – Gross Domestic Product
MVA – Manufacturing Value Added

The region's sluggish investment performance is again apparent from the per capita figures for gross fixed capital formation (GFCF) in Table 1.2. Although Japan has consistently led other industrialized regions in this field, per capita GFCF in Western Europe was more than 80 per cent of the Japanese level in 1975 and slightly higher than the US figure. The slow growth of European investment in later years led to a widening gap between the three markets. By 1984, the region's per capita investment was roughly four-fifths of the American total and less than two-thirds of the Japanese level.

Changes in the composition of GDP provide some impression of the way in which various economic sectors have fared over the course of the present economic cycle. Table 1.3 brings together data for this purpose for Western Europe and the USA. The reference years chosen for this comparison were 1979, representing the last year in the previous cyclical peak in Western Europe, the trough year of 1982, and 1985, the latest year for which comparable data were available. The brunt of the decline in 1979–82 was borne by the manufacturing and construction sectors. The relative contraction in the two sectors was most severe in the USA. Sectoral shifts during the subsequent recovery (1982–85) yield further contrasts. Manufacturing rebounded quickly in the USA. That sector accounted for one-third of the growth in GDP while two-thirds of the gains are attributable to services. In West Europe the sources of growth were more equally distributed between services and manufacturing.

TABLE 1.3   SECTORAL CONTRIBUTION TO CHANGES IN TOTAL GDP
I. Cumulative change in per cent;
II. Percentage contribution to total change

| Sector | Western Europe | | | | United States | | | |
| | 1979–1982 | | 1982–1985 | | 1979–1982 | | 1982–1985 | |
	I	II	I	II	I	II	I	II
Agriculture	12.0	+38	2.8	+1	13.4	+150	5.2	+1
Mining, utilities	0.3	0	10.1	+10	2.9	+50	4.7	+1
Manufacturing	−3.4	−78	7.5	+35	−8.3	−850	19.1	+32
Construction	−5.6	−30	−4.0	−3	−16.0	−250	14.1	+4
Services	3.8	+123	7.3	+51	3.9	+950	15.3	+61
Government sector	4.7	+46	2.9	+7	2.1	+100	1.7	+1
Total output change (per cent)	1.3	100	6.0	100	0.2	100	13.8	100

Source: ECE, OECD and author's calculations
Note: Figures may not add up to total because of rounding

A significant portion of the manufacturing gains reported in both the USA and West Europe during the recovery has served merely to offset the sector's earlier decline. In contrast, the performance of services proved to be less sensitive to cyclical factors. The effects of macroeconomic policy can also be inferred from the data. The recovery of manufacturing and the continued expansion of services in the USA proceeded at a more rapid pace than in West Europe, a distinction which was largely due to the stimulative fiscal policies adopted in the American economy. The overall impression conveyed by these figures is that the sectoral patterns of change were similar in both areas with US growth depending somewhat more heavily on the service sector than was true for West Europe.

III   Comparative economic performance

International differences of rates of output growth or patterns of structural change are not the only broad criteria for judging economic performance. Other conventional measures include the ability to control inflation, the generation of new employment opportunities and the degree of dynamism in the industrial sector. The following discussion extends the international assessment of West European performance by considering each of these elements.

A government's ability to control inflation is vital, not only to preserve the economy's competitive position in international markets but also to avoid the many types of domestic distortions which can result. In West Europe the economic recoveries of the 1960s and 1970s were characterized by rates of inflation which tended to reach successively higher levels. However, the continued deceleration of inflation distinguishes the present economic cycle from previous ones. Whether measured according to the GDP deflator or in terms of consumer prices, rates of inflation in West Europe declined in 1986 for the sixth consecutive year.

All European governments have adopted moderate-to-stringent anti-inflationary policies. The impact of these programmes was reinforced by several economic developments. During the first two years of present recovery, most currencies appreciated against the dollar with the result that import prices, when expressed in local currencies, fell. Declining commodity prices – in particular the price of oil – helped to reduce the price of inputs. Another factor contributing to the easing of inflationary pressures has been a moderate rise in labour productivity (see Chapter 4) which has dampened the growth of unit labour costs in Western Europe. Finally, diminished inflationary expectations coupled with rising levels of unemployment have tempered the growth of wage demands in recent years.

Despite the combination of favourable economic trends and stringent government policies, West Europe's overall record on inflation does not equal that of Japan or the USA. The data in Table 1.4 show that the region's average rate of inflation surpassed that of other industrialized countries in each year during the period 1982–85. West Germany was the only large European country to achieve a degree of inflation control which matched that of Japan and the USA. In the UK, higher rates of interest and a depreciation of sterling in 1985 led to some acceleration of price levels which marred that country's anti-inflation performance. France and Italy chose to rely on income policies as a major adjunct to monetary and fiscal policies in order to reduce further their inflation rates. These tactics resulted in some improvements in 1984 and 1985 although rates of inflation were still slightly above the European average.

TABLE 1.4   INFLATION IN WESTERN EUROPE, JAPAN AND THE USA
            (percentage change)

GNP deflator	Growth rate (compound)		Annual rate of change			
	1968–77	1978–85	1982	1983	1984	1985
Western Europe	8.2	8.3	9.4	7.3	5.6	5.3
of which:						
France[a]	7.9	9.9	12.6	9.5	7.1	5.9
Italy[a]	10.9	15.2	17.8	15.0	10.7	9.0
United Kingdom[a]	11.0	10.0	7.3	5.1	4.0	6.1
West Germany	5.3	3.6	4.3	3.3	1.9	2.1
USA	6.5	6.6	6.5	3.8	4.1	3.3
Japan	8.3	2.6	1.9	0.8	1.3	1.7
Consumer prices						
Western Europe	7.8	8.4	9.5	7.3	6.1	5.3
of which:						
France	8.0	10.2	11.8	9.6	7.4	5.8
Italy	9.8	14.8	16.3	15.1	10.7	9.2
United Kingdom	11.3	9.5	8.6	4.6	5.0	6.1
West Germany	4.5	4.0	5.3	3.3	2.4	2.2
USA	6.1	7.5	6.1	3.2	4.3	3.5
Japan	9.3	3.7	2.7	1.9	2.2	2.1

Source: IMF
[a] Figures are based on GDP at market prices

European countries other than the largest ones have been less successful in containing inflation. Spanish authorities have emphasized the need to moderate wage demands in order to reduce inflation. The government established wage norms for the public sector in 1983 and expected the private sector to follow suit. After some initial rise, real wages stabilized in 1984–85. Nevertheless, Spain's rate of inflation was 9 per cent in 1985 and 1986 – nearly double the average for Western Europe. In Greece, consumer prices rose by 23 per cent in 1986 after increasing by 19 per cent in 1985. Unlike other European countries, Greece's fiscal and monetary policies have been expansionary, while the effects of a currency depreciation on domestic prices were magnified by a system of wage indexation. Inflation also accelerated in Norway, reaching 7.2 per cent in 1986, while Denmark experienced a similar upward trend during the second half of that year.

Despite these exceptions, regional averages show a sharp deceleration in the rate of inflation during 1986. Consumer prices rose by only 2.3 per cent. This was less than one-half the increase in 1985, and the lowest rate since 1961. Overall, the general pattern in West Europe has been for national differences in rates of inflation to narrow in recent years. Those countries with increases higher than average have generally achieved the most significant reductions in inflation.

Turning to the field of employment, the total number employed in Western Europe rose by 700,000 (see Table 1.5 p10) in each of the last two years. These gains represent a modest acceleration after six consecutive years in which growth had slowed. During the early part of the 1980s, the labour force of Western Europe experienced particularly drastic cuts. The numbers employed during the period 1979–83 declined at an annual average of 640,000. Reductions in workforces were generally the result of a slowdown in growth of productivity coupled with a rise in the prices of intermediate inputs. But once the economic recovery began, the numbers employed grew moderately in most countries. France, Ireland and Spain were the only countries to report employment losses in 1985 and in each case the declines were appreciably smaller than in 1984. But despite some improvement, unemployment rates remain high in several West European countries, ranging between 11 and 18 per cent in Belgium, Ireland and the Netherlands.

So long as the demand for labour is weak, the evolution of labour supply will be a major determinant of future levels of unemployment. In 1984, the labour force grew at a rate which was double that for employment, giving rise to an additional 570,000 unemployed.

TABLE 1.5   LABOUR MARKET PERFORMANCE IN WESTERN EUROPE
AND NORTH AMERICA

	Western Europe*a*			North America		
	1983–84	1984–85	1985–86	1983–84	1984–85	1985–86
Labour force						
avge annual change (in '000s)	1060	1140	850	2210	2090	2500
growth rate (per cent)	0.8	0.9	0.6	1.8	1.6	1.9
Employment						
avge annual change (in '000s)	490	690	700	4400	2440	2700
growth rate (per cent)	0.4	0.6	0.6	3.9	2.1	2.2
Unemployment						
avge annual change (in '000s)	570	340	150	−2230	−350	−200
annual average (per cent)*b*	9.4	9.7	9.6	7.8	7.4	−7.1

Source: ECE
a Includes 13 countries: Austria, Belgium, Denmark, Finland, France, Ireland, Italy,
Netherlands, Norway, Sweden, Switzerland, the United Kingdom and West
Germany

Employment growth accelerated in 1985 but again the gains did not
match additions to the labour force, and unemployment worsened. It
was not until 1986 that the region began to approach a rough balance
between growth of the labour force and employment. Moreover, this
achievement was due not so much to a surge in employment as to a
slowdown in the growth of the labour force.

The European experience contrasts markedly with that in North
America. In the latter region the number of new entrants has
substantially exceeded additions to the European labour force.
However, the fact that 6.8 million new jobs were also added in 1984
and 1985 meant that unemployment in North America fell to 7.4 per
cent. This achievement far surpassed European performance.
Depending on the definition used, the unemployment rate for all of
Western Europe ranged between 9.7 and 11.2 per cent in 1985[1]. And
regardless of which definition is adopted, European unemployment
rates have risen in every year since 1982.

Several features help to explain the comparatively poor performance of European economies in this field. With regard to the
demand for labour, many industries underwent a drastic process of
retrenchment during the first three years of this decade. The

[1]   Unemployment measures may be defined as in Table 1.5. Alternatively, they may refer only
to the civilian workforce, exclude the self-employment or be based only on those who have
registered as being unemployed.

number of jobs cut was substantial and the process was not fully completed by 1984. Furthermore, those industries which had recently experienced painful contractions were often hesitant to increase hiring their workforce once economic recovery began.

The circumstances contributing to the recent growth of the labour supply are somewhat more complex. One important characteristic has been an acceleration in the 'activity rate' (the proportion of working-age population in the labour force). After declining for several years, the activity rate began to rise in 1984. A major reason for the shift has been the growing feminization of the labour force. While the male participation rate has tended to stagnate or even fall, there has been a steady rise in female participation in the workforce. Between 1975 and 1984, growth of the female labour force exceeded that of the male workforce in all countries of West Europe other than Finland and Ireland.

A second feature of Western Europe's unemployment problem concerns the sectoral composition of the workforce. Since 1979, employment in the industrial sector has steadily declined throughout the region. During the same period, service employment has risen – albeit at a slower pace than in the 1970s. There are reasons to expect that the labour movements associated with this type of shift are more sluggish than intra-sector movements of workers. Service employment generally pays less than jobs in industry. Many service openings are only part-time. Furthermore, work conditions and other benefits in that sector are less attractive than for employment elsewhere. Unemployed industrial workers may, therefore, be reluctant to accept service employment and thus aggravate demand-supply imbalances in the labour market.

The severity of the unemployment problem is, of course, related to the overall growth performance of the region. For many, a vital and dynamic industrial sector is crucial if a country is to retain a satisfactory standard of living. West Europe, however, is often thought to offer clear evidence of de-industrialization. To the extent that industry can be regarded as 'the engine room of growth', the threat of de-industrialization is a real one. Table 1.6 (p12) provides an international comparison of industrial growth in West Europe, Japan and the USA during the 1980s. Western Europe's industrial sector faltered noticeably in 1981–83 and began to recover only slowly in 1984. As in other sectors, the contraction continued longer than in the USA or Japan. It was also widespread: there are very few European countries which did not experience a significant fall in industrial output during the early 1980s.

TABLE 1.6   GROWTH OF INDUSTRIAL PRODUCTION
(Indexes, 1980 = 100)

	1981	1982	1983	1984	1985	1986ᵃ	Growth rate, 1980–85
Western Europe	98.5	96.9	98.0	101.0	103.8	106.5	0.8
Japan	102.3	100.9	110.1	120.0	121.5	—	4.5
United States	102.2	94.3	100.6	112.1	114.5	115.2	3.0

Source: ECE, OECD
ᵃ Preliminary

Industrial production remained sluggish in 1986. For the majority of West European countries, growth in that year was less than in 1985. The latest slowdown – which was pronounced during the second half of 1986 – reflects a weaker export performance with repercussions for producers of investment goods. That sub-sector of industry had previously been the main source of output growth. However, a deterioration in overseas sales prospects reduced domestic demand for investment goods in a number of West European countries.

Recent growth performance should be seen in relation to longer-term patterns of structural change. The data in Table 1.7 show changes in the composition of MVA in West Europe, Japan and the USA. Three broad industrial groups dominate in the manufacturing sector of West Europe. A surprisingly large portion of the region's output is accounted for by the food, beverages and tobacco industries. Contrary to the experiences of either the USA or Japan, the share of agro-related industries in total MVA rose between 1975 and 1984. A second industry of major importance is chemicals. Here, again, the extent of specialization in Western Europe is somewhat greater than in either of the other two markets. Finally, the manufacture of metal products, machinery and equipment – often described as capital goods industries – accounts for the largest share of MVA in all three markets. In Europe the share of these industries has been stable since 1975. This pattern contrasts with that in Japan and the USA, where capital goods have accounted for a steadily rising share of total MVA.

TABLE 1.7   INTERNATIONAL COMPARISON OF THE COMPOSITION
OF MVA[a]
(percentage)[b]

	Western Europe		USA		Japan	
	1975	1984	1975	1984	1975	1984
Food, beverages and tobacco (31)	12.7	13.5	9.3	8.9	12.6	8.9
Textile, wearing apparel and leather (32)	9.8	8.3	6.8	5.5	7.3	5.1
Wood and wood products, excluding furniture (33)	4.5	4.1	5.1	5.4	4.5	2.4
Paper and paper products, printing and publishing (34)	6.3	7.2	9.5	10.3	7.8	6.7
Chemicals, petroleum, coal, rubber and plastic products (35)	14.3	15.1	12.8	13.9	11.6	11.3
Non-metallic mineral products, except products of petroleum and coal (36)	4.9	4.4	3.3	3.1	4.3	3.5
Basic metals (37)	7.1	6.5	9.4	6.3	13.9	11.5
Manufacture of metal products, machinery and equipment (38)	39.4	39.6	42.2	45.2	36.4	49.6
of which:						
Fabricated metal products (381)	6.3	5.9	7.5	6.8	6.9	6.0
Non-electrical machinery (382)	12.3	11.9	12.1	12.9	10.3	12.1
Electrical machinery, apparatus, appliances and supplies (383)	8.9	10.2	7.3	9.8	8.0	20.4
Transport equipment (384)	10.2	10.1	12.0	12.5	10.3	9.1
Professional, scientific, measuring and controlling equipment not elsewhere classified (385)	1.7	1.5	3.3	3.2	0.9	2.0
Other manufacturing (39)	1.3	1.4	1.6	1.4	1.3	1.2

Source: UN, UNIDO
[a] Expressed in constant US dollars at 1980 prices
[b] Sum of branches do not add up to 100 per cent due to rounding

The impression which emerges from this comparison is that Western Europe is relatively specialized in industries which, for various reasons, are comparatively slow-growing fields of manufacturing. In the case of agro-related industries, the growth constraints imposed through market saturation and low income elasticities are well known. Chemicals is an energy-intensive industry which was especially hard hit by the rise in oil prices in the 1970s and the subsequent emergence of large tracts of new capacity in OPEC countries. Industries producing capital goods have provided the major source of industrial growth in Japan and the USA but have not played the same role in Western Europe.

In conclusion, the broad outlines of industrial growth and structural change in the three markets provide several contrasts between West Europe and its international rivals. Though industrial growth in West Europe had resumed by 1984 and even accelerated in 1985, performance has fallen far short of that in Japan or the USA. Meanwhile, changes in the composition of MVA suggest somewhat different patterns of growth in Western Europe which cannot be readily attributed to demand or consumer preferences but are more likely the result of underlying differences in policy and supply characteristics.

IV   Involvement in the world trading system

The extent to which West European economies depend on international trade has long been one of the region's distinguishing economic features. There are obvious reasons – both economic and institutional – for the important role of trade. Because most European countries have relatively small domestic markets, they rely heavily on foreign markets and suppliers. The existence of the EC and the European Free Trade Association (EFTA) provide an institutional framework conducive to international trade that is unmatched in any other region in the world. While these arrangements fall short of genuine market integration, they ensure that international trade will remain a centrepiece of European economies.

The data in Table 1.8 provide the basis for an international comparison of trade patterns in Western Europe, the USA and Japan. Unlike the USA or Japan, the region has never had a serious trade imbalance: imports have tended to exceed exports, but the difference between the two has not been great. A more dramatic contrast is found in the total size of each trade flow in the three markets. In 1985, the EC alone accounted for one-third of the world's exports of goods and services while the corresponding share for all Western Europe was 39 per cent. With regard to exports, Europe's growth has moderately surpassed that of the USA but is far less impressive than that of Japan. The value of West Europe's

TABLE 1.8   AN INTERNATIONAL COMPARISON OF TRADE PATTERNS 1975–85

	USA				Japan			
	1975	1985	1986[b]	Growth rate 1975–85	1975	1985	1986[b]	Growth rate 1975–85
Exports								
Value (bnUS$)	108.1	213.1	217.3	(7.0)	55.8	175.7	155.5	(12.1)
Share in world (percentage)	12.3	11.0	10.3	—	6.4	9.1	10.0	—
Imports								
Value (bnUS$)	105.9	361.6	375.6	(13.1)	57.9	129.5	96.1	(8.4)
Share in world (percentage)	11.7	17.7	17.8	—	6.4	6.3	5.8	—

	Western Europe[a]				of which, EC			
	1975	1985	1986[b]	Growth rate 1975–85	1975	1985	1986[b]	Growth rate 1975–85
Exports								
Value (bnUS$)	359.1	752.2	644.6	(7.7)	306.4	639.4	—	(7.6)
Share in world (percentage)	40.9	38.8	30.5	—	34.9	33.0	—	—
Imports								
Value (bnUS$)	384.1	771.4	631.5	(7.2)	322.8	657.7	—	(7.3)
Share in world (percentage)	42.3	37.7	29.9	—	35.7	32.1	—	—

	World			
	1975	1985	1986[b]	Growth rate 1975–85
Exports				
Value (bnUS$)	877.1	1938.2	211.0	(8.3)
Share in world (percentage)	100.0	100.0	100.0	—
Imports				
Value (bnUS$)	907.1	2045.9	211.0	(8.5)
Share in world (percentage)	100.0	100.0	100.0	—

[a] Includes intra-European trade
[b] Figures for 1986 are preliminary. They have been constructed from a trade matrix in which, by definition, total exports equals total imports. Official trade statistics, however, often yield a discrepancy between the two trade flows which may range from $5 to $50 billion per year
Source: UN, ECE and GATT

15

exports in 1975 was more than twice that of Japan and the USA combined. Ten years later, the region's exports were still far greater than those of the other two countries. The data for imports reflect a similar set of relationships. In West Europe imports have grown slowly, although the value of this trade flow is much larger than the totals reported for Japan and the USA.

Western Europe's trade relations with the rest of the world are somewhat more volatile and sensitive to change than the foregoing figures would suggest. Table 1.9 shows the growth of trade with other markets in 1984 and 1985. The evidence, however, should be viewed in light of the fact that the bulk of the region's trade is intra-European. In 1985, trade with the rest of the world amounted to less than 35 per cent of Western Europe's total trade. Bearing this qualification in mind, the data reveal some significant shifts in trade patterns.

TABLE 1.9   GROWTH OF WESTERN EUROPEAN TRADE
WITH OTHER REGIONS
(percentage change over preceding year)

Region[a]	Imports		Exports	
	1984	1985	1984	1985
North America	1.7	1.1	25.3	13.2
Asia	7.6	1.9	7.3	12.4
Africa	4.9	7.7	−4.3	−5.7
Eastern Europe	3.9	−7.4	−5.8	3.0
Middle East	−12.2	−13.8	−11.4	−11.6
Latin America	2.7	2.5	2.7	0.4

Source: GATT
[a] Ranked in descending order of share of Western Europe's exports in 1985

Although the growth of exports to North America was almost halved in 1985, that market continued to be the most rapidly growing source of foreign demand for European producers. The deceleration in the US economy apparently had no negative impact on Western Europe's overall export performance. This result can be attributed to the especially strong growth in American import demand and the fact that Europe's exports to the USA represent less than 10 per cent of the region's total exports (including intra-European trade).

Asian markets took on added importance in 1985 as West Europe's exports to that region grew almost as rapidly as those to North America. Because of hard currency shortages and political constraints, Western Europe's shipments to Eastern Europe had fallen during most of the 1980s. However, these impediments were not so severe in 1985 and the region's exports to the Eastern bloc rose by 3 per cent. The importance of Middle Eastern markets continued to wane as oil prices fell. That region's share of West European exports had risen dramatically in the 1970s following each of the two major hikes in petroleum prices. But by 1985, exports to the Middle East had dropped back to levels prevailing in the mid-1970s. Owing to high levels of international debt, European exports to several Third World countries in Africa and Latin America grew very little or even contracted in 1985. Among other markets, the case of China should be noted. Western Europe's exports to that country rose by 75 per cent in 1985 – mainly due to the performance of suppliers in West Germany and France.

Western Europe's imports from the rest of the world reveal a distinctly different picture. Between 1984 and 1985 the growth of imports rose in only one case, that of Africa. Imports from North America and Asia grew only slightly in 1985. With the fall in oil prices, West European imports from both communist countries and the Middle East declined. This performance by non-European suppliers was in marked contrast to intra-European trade (not shown), which grew by 6.9 per cent in 1985.

V International economic relations

The types of interdependence which link West European economies with other parts of the world are largely shaped by the region's ties with the USA. At present, two issues dominate international policy discussions between representatives of the two markets. These concern protectionism and an interrelated set of disputes involving the international value of the dollar, with implications for monetary and fiscal policy.

With regard to the first of these issues, the extravagantly protectionist policies of the EC in agricultural products appear to be a major cause of recurrent disagreement. These policies have led to dramatic increases in European farm output and high surpluses at a time when the American producers are losing their premier position in world food markets. Protectionist disputes in the field of manufacturing have been only slightly less divisive. The most prominent of these involves the steel industry. After a long-lasting dispute with a series of protectionist tactics including charges of price dumping, export restraints, marketing agreements, quotas and other trade restraints, the USA and the EC concluded a steel pact to govern trade until 1988. While trade in steel has been the subject of such heated protectionist disputes, other recent ones include maize, sorghum, supersonic aircraft and machine tools.

The protectionist problem is made worse by the way European and American negotiators have tried to resolve trade disputes. Disagreements are routinely settled with bilateral quotas and market-sharing agreements. Such restrictions now affect more than one-third of West Europe's imports from the USA. Settlements of this type, however, are 'communicable', meaning that they are quickly extended to include a growing range of related products and new sources of supply.

Wide fluctuations in the value of the dollar have tended to exacerbate the protectionist problem under the present system of floating exchange rates. Europeans have traditionally been reluctant to accept a system of floating exchange rates. In the late 1970s the EC responded to the dollar's slide by creating the European Monetary System (EMS) to provide 'a zone of monetary stability'. When the dollar began to fall in 1985–86, the EMS came under renewed pressure, making policy co-ordination within the EC even more complicated.

The reasons why Europeans favour fixed exchange rates are straightforward. More than one-half of Europe's exports are sold within the region and the bulk of these goods are manufactures. Because of these features, Europeans compete mainly on the basis of labour costs when they trade. With the exception of the few European energy exporters, intra-European trade is little affected by commodity prices. Such homogeneity makes it important for exchange rates to reflect differentials in production costs. When they do not, high-inflation countries become less competitive and more prone to protectionist appeals. In practise, floating exchange rates have frequently failed to accomodate intra-European shifts in competitiveness. Because of overshooting, a currency often appreciates even though industrial costs are rising faster than average.

The opportunities for removing this source of tension between Americans and Europeans in this field seem to be limited. The world has now discarded its system of fixed exchange rates. The vague system of 'reference ranges' established in early 1987 has steadily become more precarious. A collapse of the dollar would not only bring renewed pressure on the EMS but would also fuel protectionist campaigns. Any attempt by the Europeans to create their own international currency is certain to bring objections from US negotiators, but in the long-run, this may prove to be the only way to accommodate the fundamentally different needs of the two regions.

The US dollar's fall against the yen has obscured the associated implications for Western Europe. Despite the yen-dollar realignment, its relation with European currencies has changed very little. Because Japanese-European exchange rates have remained comparatively stable, the trade equation between the world's three major markets has changed. There is some fear (among Europeans) that patterns of international trade may be altered. Japanese exporters may be inclined to turn their attention from the USA to Europe. Certainly, Japanese companies now have a greater incentive to export to Western Europe, where every unit sold maximizes profits in yen. The new currency relationships could result in a deterioration in West Europe's balance of trade with Japan, erasing many of the Europeans' recent export gains in that market.

Although the EC has begun to monitor Japanese imports to determine whether trade diversion is occurring, European officials have played down the possibility of new restraints. There are several reasons why the EC would want to avoid any deterioration in its trading relations with Japan. One is that European markets have not been penetrated by Japanese goods to the extent the USA has. Another reason is that European countries – because they are far more dependent on trade than the USA – are anxious to avoid any mutually damaging sanctions. Europeans have also been more successful in gaining entry to the Japanese market than American companies. Finally, Japan is seen by many Europeans as the new world's source of direct and indirect investment in much the same way as OPEC countries were in the 1970s.

West Europe's economic relations with Eastern Europe constitute another important element in its network of international links. In that case, the dominant features involve the inter-related elements of trade, finance and energy. With regard to trade, West Europe is the largest hard-currency market for Soviet exports as well as the major supplier of western goods. In turn, Western Europe's imports from the Eastern bloc depend mainly on developments in the energy sphere. Because more than one-quarter of all Eastern Europe's exports to Western Europe consist of oil and gas, East-West trade is especially sensitive to movements in energy prices. In the first nine months of 1986, the average price of Eastern Europe's hard currency exports of energy fell by 35 per cent compared with the same period in 1985. An increase in the volume of the Eastern bloc's energy exports to the West only partially offsets this decline.

Eastern Europe's ability to import from Western Europe is mainly constrained by a shortage of hard currency. This limitation, in turn, is largely a result of the Eastern bloc's inability to maintain its earnings from energy exports. In 1985, Western Europe's exports to the East grew following a substantial increase in the latter countries' borrowing in international markets. In general, however, the volatility of energy prices and the slow pace of further development of Soviet energy supplies have created considerable uncertainty with regard to East-West trade and undermined the links between the two regions.

The Soviet Union's pronounced policy of 'openness' would seem to hold out opportunities for trade between East and West Europe. Optimists see the new initiative as promising a substantial boost to trade. However, financial limitations will continue to be a major constraint. Eastern importers are simply unable to afford a significant increase in their purchases from West Europe. Rather than leading to a significant increase in the Soviet bloc's imports from West Europe, a more likely outcome would be a shift in the composition of goods traded. The Soviet government's intention to reform its trading system to allow for more direct deals and joint ventures with foreign firms should hasten a change in the composition of the Eastern bloc's trade with West Europe. This could make it easier for Soviet industries to obtain the types of Western goods and machinery they need and allow them a better chance of selling non-energy products. Any relaxation in the West's strategic trade controls on exports to the USSR would also mean that Western European suppliers of capital goods and other high-tech products would have new opportunities to export to the East.

CHAPTER TWO
THE EUROPEAN COMMUNITY:
ITS ECONOMIC ROLE IN EUROPE TODAY

I Introduction

Of all the major organizations linking West European countries, few have generated such consistent criticism, frustration or admiration as the European Community. Formed in a burst of federalistic enthusiasm during the 1950s, the Community (and especially the European Economic Community, or EEC) has certainly fallen well short of the ambitious central aim of its founders – the creation of a unified European system involving not only a common market for goods and services but also a common currency, an integrated and self-complementary infrastructure, a pooling of industrial and technological resources and, ultimately, some form of political union. Progress has been hampered by the fears of its member states about losing any part of their national sovereignty to what would be, after all, an amalgam of often conflicting interests, with all the power to change things but none of the responsibility if they were to go wrong.

But if the rather daunting goals of its founders seem far away in the late 1980s, the catalogue of achievements has been impressive as well. The EEC has been the model and the inspiration for similar common markets in south-east Asia, in Latin America and the Caribbean, and in Africa. It has managed to harmonize conflicting standards in a large number of fields; it has tried to iron out the worst discrepancies in standards of living through such agencies as its regional development fund, and through guarantees of job mobility and the right of settlement. Lastly, and most importantly, it has fulfilled its most basic brief of ensuring that demand is covered, and it has orchestrated its heavy industries (if not, by any means, its farmers) so as to combat surpluses of basic production.

Meanwhile, the regular meetings of EEC leaders have transformed the European Council into a powerful and broad-based forum within which world affairs in general can be discussed, and in the mid-1980s the Community has found itself speaking increasingly with one voice on international issues. It has taken on Japan and the United States over trade issues, in a way which would have been unthinkable without the strength of its union. It has adopted joint policies on terrorism, drugs, medical questions, apartheid, disaster relief, aid to developing countries, and the global environment. Finally, it has been a support to the North Atlantic Treaty Organisation, and the meetings of its leaders were instrumental in persuading Spain to stay in NATO when the issue came to a national referendum in March 1986.

As the Community's influence has grown, so has its ability to attract new members from among neighbouring countries. The original complement of six members (France, West Germany, Italy, Belgium, Luxembourg and the Netherlands) had swelled to twelve by 1987 with the inclusion of Britain, Ireland and Denmark (1973), Greece (1981), and Spain and Portugal (1986). In 1986 the EEC could claim to speak for 320 million consumers, the largest unified market in the industrialized world. In April 1987 Turkey (population 55 million) also made a formal bid for membership of the Community, having for many years been an associate member, and Morocco and Malta subsequently declared their intentions to apply.

II   Political structure and organization

The European Community has its origins in the European Coal and Steel Community (ECSC), whose charter was signed in 1951 by the six founder members, France, West Germany, Belgium, Luxembourg, Italy and the Netherlands. The ECSC succeeded within three years in its primary aim of removing internal barriers in the coal, coke, steel, pig-iron and scrap iron businesses; it went on to play a major part in the reorganization of the European coal and steel business during the early 1980s, exercising powers to fine member countries which broke its regulations and awarding financial assistance for retraining and resettlement.

The European Economic Community itself came into being,

along with the European Atomic Energy Community (Euratom), on 25th March, 1957. The Treaty of Rome, which is effectively the Community's constitution, came into effect on 1st January, 1958, and it has remained the driving force behind Community policy. The EEC has observer status at the United Nations and at such other international organizations as the World Bank, and it maintains diplomatic relations in its own right with some 108 countries.

Since 1967 the ECSC, the EEC and Euratom have shared one European Commission and one European Council instead of maintaining separate administrations. Administrative work is managed by staffs based in Brussels (the technically temporary home of the European Commission), in Strasbourg (the *de facto* home of the ECJ) and in Luxembourg (the seat of the European Parliament).

The Treaty of Rome was aimed ultimately at a complete political union of its member states, a proposition which, as we have noted, has fallen somewhat by the wayside over the years; but in the interim its goal was to establish a common market, and in the words of Article 2, 'to promote throughout the Community a harmonious development of economic activities, a continuous and balanced expansion, an increase in stability, an accelerated raising of the standard of living and closer relations between the states belonging to it'. Some of the detailed implications for trade, both internal and external, are examined below.

The European Commission is the main source of policy within the European Community. Although it has no absolute powers to enact legislation, its function is to start the decision-making process by making proposals (known as directives) to the Council of Ministers; it may also issue recommendations to the Council and to the European Parliament, which are not in themselves binding. In practice the Commission's powers are somewhat more extensive than this would suggest; the European Parliament would find itself in very deep water if it opposed a major Commission recommendation for very long.

The Commission's other main responsibility is to help implement decisions adopted by the Council of Ministers, and to ensure compliance with international treaties to which the Community is a party. Its 17 members act independently of their national governments; in 1987, it comprised two members each from the United Kingdom, West Germany, Italy, France and Belgium, as well as one member each from the Netherlands, Spain, Portugal, Greece, Ireland, Denmark and Luxembourg.

The principal decision-making body in the European Community is the Council of Ministers, also based in Brussels; it considers the directives issued by the European Commission and makes recommendations to the European Parliament, whose approval is required in most instances. The Council has no fixed composition but may comprise any relevant ministerial representatives of the member states, according to the topic under discussion. It is chaired by the President of the Council of Ministers, who is appointed on a rotating basis for a six-month term of office, in a sequence which follows the alphabetical order of names among the member states.

Not having a fixed membership, the Council relies heavily on its Committee of Permanent Representatives (Coreper), which attends to preparatory work in collaboration with officials in the member states. The Council acts either by issuing regulations, which are binding on member states, or through non-binding recommendations like those of the Commission.

The powers of the Council are to be substantially enhancèd under the Single European Act, which is outlined in a subsequent section. Votes in the Council correspond roughly to population size, and in 1987 the United Kingdom, France, West Germany and Italy each controlled ten of the 76 votes while Spain had eight, Belgium, Greece, Portugal and the Netherlands had five, Denmark and Ireland had three, and Luxembourg had two votes. Under the conditions prevailing at the start of 1987, 54 votes were required for a qualified majority but only 23 votes for a blocking minority. In theory, it has always been possible to carry a motion on a majority decision, but in cases where the national interests of a member are at stake, it is usual to argue the case out until complete agreement has been reached. In such cases, abstentions by member states do not prevent the adoption of a resolution.

The European Parliament, based in Luxembourg, is composed of directly-elected members who, although they represent their countries' interests, also divide themselves into political blocs within the Community. They serve for a term of five years, and those of all countries except Spain and Portugal were last elected in 1984; the Spanish and Portuguese deputies have been directly appointed by their respective political parties. Strictly speaking, the European Parliament has no legislative powers at all, although it can reject or

TABLE 2.1   COMPOSITION OF GROUPINGS IN THE EUROPEAN PARLIAMENT, 1987

	Socialists	European People's Party	European Democrats	Communists	Liberal & Democratic Reformists	European Alliance for Renewal & Democracy	Rainbow Group (mainly regional & ecology)	European Right	Independents	Total
Belgium	8	6	—	—	5	—	4	—	1	24
Denmark	3	1	4	2	2	—	4	—	—	16
West Germany	33	41	—	—	—	—	7	—	—	81
Spain	36	7	13	—	2	—	1	—	1	60
Greece	10	8	—	4	—	—	—	1	1	24
France	20	10	—	10	11	20	—	10	—	81
Ireland	—	6	—	—	1	8	—	—	—	15
Italy	12	27	—	27	5	—	2	5	3	81
Luxembourg	2	3	—	—	1	—	—	—	—	6
Netherlands	9	8	—	—	5	1	2	—	—	25
Portugal	6	2	—	3	9	4	—	—	—	24
United Kingdom	33	—	46	—	—	1	—	—	1	81
Total strength	172	119	63	46	41	34	20	16	7	518

Source: European Commission

modify the European Community budget and it can also give opinions to the European Council concerning proposals put forward by the European Commission. Like the Council, however, it stands to gain greater powers under the Single European Act.

The European Council is the summit-level organ of the Community, comprising the President and one Vice-President of the European Commission, as well as the prime ministers and foreign ministers of the member states (or, in France's case, the president and foreign minister). It meets three times a year and, while exercising no formal powers, it has been especially important in co-ordinating the workings of the European Monetary System (EMS), in negotiating the European Budget, and in talks on collective foreign policy, terrorism and trade issues.

The European Court of Justice, based in Luxembourg, is the supreme arbiter of Community law, and its thirteen judges exercise final and binding powers over member states. The court may be approached either by individuals or by governments, and it rules on the legitimacy of Community legislation, on matters of national compliance with Community law, and on various consumer matters; it is not to be confused, however, with the European Court of Human Rights in Strasbourg, which is outside the European Community.

III   The Community's economic role within Europe

The EEC functions within Western Europe principally as a common (but not yet unified) internal market for goods and services, and as we shall shortly see it does its best to simplify both production and distribution of both manufactured and agricultural goods, as well as promoting industrial co-operation and exchanging opinions on matters of joint general interest, including finance and infra-structure.

The Community also incorporates defensive mechanisms against aggressive or undercutting market policies from abroad, and it has powers to levy import duties aimed at raising the price of cheap non-EEC imports to the level where they compare with EEC-produced goods. It can subsidize exports of high-cost European goods, so as to attain similar levels of parity for European goods on international markets, and in some cases it imposes import quotas backed up by threats of countervailing duties.

The Treaty of Rome envisages the eventual creation of a unified monetary system in Europe; originally, this was intended to be a single European currency, but in practice the Community has had to settle for a system which merely links the existing national currencies. The European Monetary System, established in March 1979, has been highly successful in limiting exchange rate movements within the Community, and in thus reducing the day-to-day volatility of currencies. By 1987, all EEC members except the United Kingdom, Greece, Spain and Portugal belonged to the EMS.

Essentially, the EMS establishes a central exchange rate for each currency. Countries are required to keep their commercial rates within a predetermined range of this central rate by buying or selling foreign reserves as appropriate. Periodically, it has been necessary to adjust the central rates so as to take account of long-term fluctuations in national economies, and these adjustments have occurred rather more often than originally intended; there were eight between 1979 and the spring of 1987, in which the Belgian and (latterly) the French currencies tended to fall while the German rate tended to rise.

The European Currency Unit (ecu) is the nearest the Community has got to a common European currency. It is intended as a medium for settling debts between consenting partners in the Community, as a form of national monetary reserve (like, say, the International Monetary Fund's Special Drawing Rights), and, theoretically, also as a means of cash payment. The ecu's value varies according to the movements of a basket of European currencies (including, incidentally, sterling and the Greek drachma). It has, however, been slow to gain acceptance even among its most ardent proponents; when Belgium issued a 50-ecu coin in early 1987, France and the United Kindgom declared it a collector's item and not a coin, and levied VAT on it.

The European Community Budget has proved over the years to be a perennial source of dispute, particularly among those countries which disapprove of the free-spending CAP. The Community finances the budget by means of a fixed percentage of VAT (currently 1.4 percentage points), and by imposing import levies on goods from outside the community. It does not issue bonds or other securities, although there is theoretically no reason why it should not.

Each year's budget is agreed by a long process of discussion between the European Commission (which presents the draft budget), the Council of Ministers (which adopts the draft) and the European Parliament (which is required to give it two readings). Debate is often acrimonious, and it is common for the year in question to be well advanced before its budget gets through; in such cases the provisions of the previous year are extended on a monthly basis until agreement ('concertation') has been reached.

IV   Key current policies

The Common Agricultural Policy (CAP) is by far the largest single activity of the European Community, accounting for between 60 and 70 per cent of the annual EEC budget. Established by the Treaty of Rome, its original aim was to increase the productivity of the farming sector and to ensure stable supplies to the market at stable prices; in particular, it aimed to improve efficiency by promoting and funding technological progress, by stressing the increased efficiency of both labour and raw materials used, and by helping to ensure a rational and balanced growth of the various sectors of the farming business.

In fact, of course, the CAP has succeeded only too well in the first of these aims while completely missing its target in the latter. By concentrating on questions of cash remuneration for producers, rather than on the requirements of the market, the CAP has generated a somewhat topheavy situation in which farmers, coaxed by subsidies into producing more and more, have achieved such excesses of some agricultural products that their very disposal has become a problem. In the process, the CAP has quite seriously antagonized many of those countries which benefit least from its generosity, and it has also been accused by environmentalists of encouraging an indiscriminate choice of crops which impoverishes certain soils and destroys hedgerows, etc., to the detriment of wildlife.

Minimum commodity prices for producers are fixed each year, on the advice of the European Commission, for about 70 per cent of all agricultural goods; daily adjustments are then made in accordance with the movement of 'green currencies', which may diverge from market exchange rates, and Monetary Compensatory Amounts (MCAs) are used to make further adjustments for price differentials at intra-EEC frontiers. Member governments and the Community itself are obliged to buy in stocks whenever market prices cross the official thresholds, and the resulting surpluses are stored in Community-funded warehouses.

The CAP has been under sharp scrutiny since around 1984, however, and the introduction of milk production quotas in that year has helped to reduce the stockpiles of dairy goods. Other surpluses have been sold at cheap rates to developing countries, to the Soviet Union or, in 1986/87, to pensioners and other welfare claimants within the EEC – a measure avoided hitherto, for fear of undermining the pricing structure.

Fisheries are controlled under the Common Fisheries Policy, which has been in force since 1983. The policy limits members to the Total Allowable Catches (TACs) specified for each of the main edible species, of which each fishing country receives an allocation. Member states are themselves responsible for enforcing the rules.

The entry of Portugal and Spain in January 1986 aroused fears in France, Italy and Greece about the increased competition for their wine, olive oil, fruit and fishing industries. Indeed, the accession of the two countries increased the EEC's farming workforce by 25 per cent and the number of fishing boats by 80 per cent. A system of gradual integration was agreed, however, under which the market was given between seven and ten years to adjust to the new conditions resulting from their entry.

The Community's industrial restructuring policy has, on the whole, been a less noisy and a more successful affair than the CAP. The EEC has achieved quite dramatic reductions of output in certain heavy industries, notably steel and shipbuilding, where there was a gross over-supply. It has done this by imposing production quotas and by enforcing them with fines on member governments; at the same time it has sought to soften the blows of plant closures by offering development grants for restructuring, retraining and redeployment of displaced staff.

Table 2.2 (p30) shows dramatically the decline in steel production which was achieved between 1979 and 1985 as a result of action by the European Commission; steel production quotas were dismantled in 1986, as a slight rise in demand permitted their relaxation.

TABLE 2.2   EUROPEAN COMMUNITY STEEL PRODUCTION, 1979–1985

Unit: million tonnes. Excluding Spain and Portugal	1979	1981	1983	1985
Belgium	13.4	12.3	10.2	10.7
Denmark	0.6	0.6	0.5	0.5
West Germany	46.0	41.6	35.7	40.5
Greece	0.8	0.9	0.9	0.1
France	23.4	21.2	17.6	18.8
Ireland	0.0	0.0	0.1	0.2
Italy	24.3	24.8	21.8	23.6
Luxembourg	5.0	3.8	3.3	3.9
Netherlands	5.8	5.5	4.5	5.5
United Kingdom	21.5	15.3	15.0	15.6
Total, incl. others	141.1	126.0	109.6	119.4

Source: European Commission

TABLE 2.3   EUROPEAN COMMUNITY STEELMAKING WORKFORCE, 1977–1986

Unit: thousands. Excluding Greece, Spain and Portugal	1977	1982	1984	Jan 1986
Belgium	54	43	40	34
Denmark	2	2	2	2
West Germany	214	181	162	150
France	149	96	90	75
Ireland	1	1	1	1
Italy	97	95	87	68
Luxembourg	20	13	13	13
Netherlands	22	21	19	19
United Kingdom	182	79	64	59
Total, incl. others	743	530	476	420

Source: European Commission/Euromonitor

Integral to the European industrial restructuring effort is the European Regional Development Fund, which aims to help all chronically depressed areas of the Community. Initiated in March 1975, it currently accounts for between 7.5 and 9 per cent of the EEC budget. Between 1975 and 1984, over 85 per cent of funds went to Italy, the UK, France and Greece; the biggest per capita recipient of regional development aid was Ireland. The Fund's brief covers a wide range of activities, including infrastructural improvements, industrial development and, in some cases, the growth of service industries.

Since 1984, when the first long-term framework for research and development was launched, the Community has increased its efforts to promote agricultural and industrial competitiveness, to reduce energy dependence and to stimulate the exchange of information on a wide range of topics. Meanwhile, work has continued on the Joint European Torus (JET), an experimental nuclear reactor at Culham, in the UK, as part of a Ecu 690 million programme of research into thermonuclear fusion.

Since 1984 the Community has also been collaborating with EFTA (see below) and with its aspiring member Turkey on such cross-border projects such as Eureka, which aims to develop commercial products and services. Other programmes in progress include Esprit, the strategic programme for research and development in information technology; the EEC offers to fund up to half of any eligible project if two or more member states are collaborating on it.

The EEC does what it can to alleviate the problem of unemployment, exchanging information on job vacancies, on the promotion of self employment and small businesses, and on improvements in job training. But on the whole, the problem is left largely with national governments. The Community is more visibly active on the issue of sex equality, and has taken issue with pension schemes, and especially with the British government, over retirement ages and the treatment of women by insurance companies.

The Community has been active in promoting common environmental policies on a range of issues, including acid rain and lead pollution. New regulations will force changes to car exhausts between 1988 and 1994, and lead-free petrol is to be made available in all member countries by 1989. In 1985 the Council of Ministers gave member states until March 1988 to conduct environmental impact studies on all planned industrial/infrastructural projects.

The Treaty of Rome provides for a common transport policy within the Community, but progress so far has been slow to say the least. There has, however, been a plan for the harmonization of axle weight limits for lorries, which is due for full implementation by 1992. Rules are also being eased regarding the issue of road haulage permits, which it is hoped will eliminate the need for some lorries to return to their bases empty.

The European Community has consistently opposed what it terms price-fixing among major airlines on European routes, but by mid

1987 it had made little progress in its efforts to force a review. The EEC had, at least, managed to open up the market for shipping – although there was to be no end to cabotage, the practice whereby member states restrict national carriage between their own ports to their own ships.

Since 1967, when the Yaoundé convention came into force, the Community has developed its trading links with developing countries through a succession of assistance programmes. Under the Lome III arrangement of 1984, 99 per cent of all production from the 64 participating countries is allowed duty-free entry to the Community. The Community guarantees minimum purchase prices for sugar and other commodities, and it also co-ordinates investments in developing countries and offers both infrastructural and emergency aid. Some of the latter takes the form of food supplies drawn from EEC stockpiles.

V   Foreign policy

Since the mid-1970s the Community has moved away from the rather bland and non-committal foreign policy stances favoured at its inception, and has played an increasingly important role in the discussion of world affairs. The EEC was instrumental in the convening of the 1975 Helsinki Conference on Human Rights; in 1980 it issued a declaration on self-determination for the Palestinians and condemned the Soviet occupation of Afghanistan; in 1981 came statements on military rule in Poland and in Turkey, and in 1982 the United Kingdom obtained its rather grudging support against Argentina in the Falklands dispute. More recent examples have included measures in 1986 against South Africa, in protest at the maintenance of apartheid, and joint action against Syria and Libya, in the wake of terrorist activities sponsored by the Syrian embassy in London.

Relations with the United States have become increasingly strained during the 1980s, as Washington has accused the EEC of subsidizing steel and agricultural produce to the detriment of the USA's trade deficit. In 1986, for example, the Reagan administration briefly imposed import quotas and heavy duties on certain EEC food products in protest at the CAP, which it said was depriving it of a $1,000 million food export market in Spain and Portugal. The Community has responded with complaints that a recent Japan-US deal on limiting computer component sales to the USA was in breach of international trade rules, and that it deflected Japanese production on to the European market. During the period of military rule in Poland, strains arose with the USA over its ban on West European sales of American-licensed computer products to Eastern Europe – a move which the EEC saw as imposing on the sovereignty of its own trading companies.

Relations with Japan have also been difficult, and in the 1980s the EEC has repeatedly taken action to protect its domestic markets from the influx of Japanese products. Tokyo's exports to EEC members totalled $21,000 million in 1985, raising the Japanese trade surplus by $300 million to $13,000 million. Japan has in the past given EEC voluntary undertakings to limit sales of certain goods, including televisions and cars, but the Community has imposed steep tariffs on photocopiers, typewriters, video recorders and other items.

At the same time, the EEC has maintained pressure on Japan to open up its own markets to European companies. Especially important to Europe are the Japanese communications and financial services markets, but other goods over which the Community has taken action have included spirits, which attract punitively high tariffs in Japan. Fears have also been expressed that Japan is circumventing the EEC's import restrictions on finished goods by setting up plants in the Community, in which Japanese components are merely bolted together with minimal local content. It was apparent in 1987 that this issue would acquire major significance as Japan increased the general level of its investment in Europe.

Not all of the Community's external relations are so defensive in character, however. The EEC maintains a strong and co-operative relationship with the European Free Trade Association (EFTA), the trading bloc to which practically all non-EEC countries in Western Europe (Austria, Iceland, Norway, Sweden, Switzerland and Finland) belong, and whose members have in the past included such EEC members as Denmark, the United Kingdom and Portugal. The two organizations maintain a range of treaties, both bilateral and multilateral, which effectively guarantee the free passage of goods between them. There is already co-operation on common trading standards and on rules of origin, and EFTA is involved in various EEC research and development projects; the Luxembourg declaration, signed in June 1986, provides for a further easing of bilateral tariffs and customs formalities between the two groups, with effect from January 1988.

Almost as important has been the role of the EEC in developing relations with the socialist countries of Eastern Europe. Members of the Council for Mutual Economic Assistance (CMEA) have consistently run trade surpluses with the EEC since 1980, but these were shrinking in 1985/86. The CMEA has been pressing a reluctant EEC to engage in jointly-negotiated multilateral trade agreements, but the Community has responded so far with the claim that bilateral agreements are more appropriate. In 1987, only Romania had any significant bilateral links with the Community.

VI Future developments

The Single European Act, signed and ratified in 1986 by all countries except Ireland (Which approved it by national referendum in 1987), is a modification of the Treaty of Rome which aims to simplify and augment the Community's decision-making process. Drawn up on the recommendation of the European Council at its June 1985 meeting in Milan, it extends the scope for majority voting in the Council of Ministers in an effort to cut through the time-consuming search for unanimity on most matters, and it extends the influence of the European Parliament – while not actually awarding additional legislative powers. The national veto of member states remains available as a last resort, however.

In the Council of Ministers, majority decisions will henceforth suffice for all issues involving national barriers to intra-Community trade, joint research and development, environmental protection, regional development policy and some monetary issues. The Council is to consult the European Parliament more closely, through a new shuttling mechanism. A new political secretariat is to co-ordinate joint foreign policy, perhaps the most significant sign of the times for the Community in the late 1980s.

Efforts have continued in the 1980s to develop the customs union established by the Treaty of Rome, but despite the absence of customs duties (abolished between 1958 and 1968), there were still major problems in 1987. These occur mainly because of differing product standards between member states, but they also reflect a stubborn refusal to harmonize the documentation of cargoes. Further obstacles derive from differences in value added tax rates; Britain, for example, was still refusing in 1987 to levy VAT on foodstuffs or on printed matter.

In June 1985 the European Council approved a White Paper prepared by the European Commission, which targeted 300 such barriers for elimination by 1992; these included differences in taxation, incompatibilities in industrial standards, and indeed the physical barriers between countries (the Commission demanding that the frontier checking of export cargoes should give way instead to a system whereby cargoes were certified and sealed by inland customs offices before beginning their journey). Progress, however, seemed slow by the autumn of 1987, and less than a third of the tasks scheduled for the first two years had been completed; even the Commission had fallen behind with its own schedule.

It has become increasingly clear in recent years that the volume of valid claims on the EEC budget is now well in excess of its ability to pay, and that some long-term increase in funding will be necessary. In February 1987 the European Commission accordingly sought a major revision of both spending and revenues in the European budget. On the expenditure side, it proposed a 33 per cent increase in outgoings for the five years to 1992; it declared that the Community should spend less on farming and more on social and regional development.

While the latter will doubtless go down well among the Community's biggest critics, the very radical character of the funding changes seems certain to arouse controversy for some years to come. Many members are aghast at what they see as a reversal of the Commission's acceptance of the previous consensus that less rather than more centralized spending should be the target for the future. The Commission has maintained that each government's contribution should be geared more closely to its ability to pay, and it has demanded a mechanism for compensating Britain for its 'excessive' net payments to the budget. Despite cutting the VAT levy from 1.4 percentage points to 1 percentage point, it hopes that the new contribution system will bring sufficient income to eliminate the Ecu 4 billion ($4.5 billion) budget deficit for 1986 at a stroke.

The EEC is moving gradually towards what it hopes will be a

completely uniform market for financial services, and since 1977 it has required member states to set minimum standards for credit institutions. In 1986 it extended the common market to insurance, and in 1987 it aimed to harmonize banks' accounts and to ensure free movement in equities. It has moved to harmonize company law and accounting practices in an effort to expedite the trend. Meanwhile, deregulation of the world stock markets has contributed in the mid-1980s to the pressure for the reform of rules governing capital movements – another main goal of the Treaty of Rome. Several restrictions on capital movements within the Community, including long-term trade credits and investments, were lifted in November 1986 – the first real change in some 25 years.

There seems little likelihood in the late 1980s, however, that the European Commission will get its way in its demand for a doubling of research and development spending in 1987–1990. The Commission would like to see total spending of over Ecu 7 billion during this period, but it has so far been consistently outvoted by the United Kingdom, France and West Germany. All of these countries, already touchy about the EEC's incursions into their industrial activities and anxious for their patent rights, have strongly voiced their favour for their own separate research programmes.

Another area of change is security. Since the mid-1980s, successive meetings of the European Council have demanded measures against the escalation of terrorism, drug trafficking and football hooliganism. In late 1986 the Community interior and justice ministers (except that of Greece, which has consistently dissociated itself from all Community initiatives on this score) agreed on a new communications network to help them track and counter terrorists and illegal weapons; proposals include closer co-operation of intelligence services, better scrutiny of diplomatic officials and, on occasions, their baggage, as well as a sharpening of extradition procedures.

CHAPTER THREE
POLITICAL AND DEFENCE ISSUES

I Introduction

The 1980s have brought a number of important and perceptible changes to the political scene in Western Europe which might have seemed surprising as recently as the early 1970s. The awareness of Europe as an economic and political entity has gained strength in many countries, as converging interests, both geographical and economic, have combined with external pressures to force West European nations together. This is not to say that there are less problems between them; it is, however, probably fair to say that there is less mistrust than in the past.

The economic crisis which followed the 1979 oil price rise has placed many European countries in a situation where their traditional post-war partner, the United States, has been unable or unwilling to help them; at the same time the rising tide of economic penetration from Japan and the Far East has helped to concentrate European minds on the need for European answers in what is clearly an atmosphere of increased economic competition. Meanwhile, there has been a significant revival of mutual trade across the Iron Curtain in recent years, accompanied by a softening of the familiar political rhetoric on both sides.

II General political trends

The mid-1970s brought a general reaffirmation of democratic principles in Western Europe, in which a succession of long-standing autocracies, actively ruling monarchies and nondemocratic political structures gave way to popular rule. The overthrow of the authoritarian regime in Portugal in 1974, the abolition of the monarchy in Greece (1973) and the subsequent removal in 1974 of the colonels who had all too quickly jumped in to replace it, and the death of General Franco in Spain (1975), together with the subsequent proclamation in 1978 of the new parliamentary democracy, were all essential stages in the attainment of broadly comparable standards of political freedom throughout Western Europe.

Of the handful of countries which maintain a true monarchy (the UK, the Netherlands, Norway, Luxembourg, Spain, Sweden and Denmark), none nowadays allows its monarch more than a nominal political role. Since the return of Turkey to parliamentary democracy in 1983, all West European countries (except Liechtenstein, where only men have the vote on national issues) now elect their national parliaments by some sort of universal adult suffrage; the voting age varies between 18 and 25, but is generally coming down to a standard of 18 years.

The early 1980s have seen a substantial shift in many countries of central and northern Europe to the political parties of the centre-right. In Britain (1979), in Norway, Denmark and the Netherlands (1981), West Germany (1982), Belgium and eventually France, such parties have gained or extended their control in government. In Italy, the socialist Bettino Craxi spent three years implementing a series of highly successful and improbably capitalist policies, before falling in mid-1987 to the more straightforwardly right-wing Giovanni Goria. In Austria, the socialist government has also survived, rather shakily, by compromising many of its left-wing ideals for the sake of regaining its economic equilibrium in the face of mounting domestic problems.

In France, too, the free-spending early years of the socialist Mitterrand administration (1981–1983) gave way to a much more conservative, austerity-dominated policy after 1983 – although even this was not enough to stop the right regaining control in 1986. Even in Sweden, the historical dominance of the left is increasingly under fire, and Finland is, in fact, the only north European country where conservatism is at bay in 1987.

In much of southern Europe, on the other hand, things have been moving to a different rhythm. As Greece, Spain and (haltingly) Portugal have entered vigorous phases of their development, the centralized systems favoured by socialist governments have been perceived as more appropriate to their needs. In Greece and Portugal, however, the state-driven development policies of the left have proved difficult to maintain – especially in view of the strong dollar and high interest rates which prevailed from 1982 to 1985 – and fairly drastic austerity measures have had to be introduced in order to regain control of the situation. It remains to be seen whether public confidence in socialism can survive these strictures, but in the autumn of 1987 the signs were still good.

With few exceptions (Portugal, Greece and Spain being the most notable examples), the successful socialist parties in Western Europe are more social democratic than far-left in character. The West German SPD in particular has in the past steered the country through many of its most remarkable economic successes; in Sweden, the Social Democrats were largely responsible for the all-embracing welfare state system which remains today; and in Spain, the socialists have presided over a period of vigorous industrial growth, brought the country into the Common Market and obtained a mandate for the country to stay in NATO.

It is less easy to draw a clear political line between right-wing and liberal parties in Europe, because they tend to cover a broader political spectrum than their socialist or social democratic adversaries. The British Conservative Party, for example, belongs well to the right in comparison with most of its EEC partners, whereas the West German Christian Democrats place considerably more emphasis on social priorities than many of their liberal rivals. European right-wing and liberal groups are, however, unanimously in favour of the free-market economy, and they all perceive the creation of wealth through private enterprise to be the greatest single factor behind economic progress.

While the smaller political groupings have generally done less well in the 1980s than in the preceding decade, the growth of environmentalist parties has been both impressive and politically important in central and northern Europe. Generally speaking, their widespread appeal derives from two main political platforms: their demands for multilateral and (generally) unilateral nuclear disarmament, and their vocal opposition to a range of environmentally controversial practices, including industrial pollution, the construction of nuclear power plants (especially fast-breeder reactors), certain modern agricultural techniques, the destruction of landscapes and the degeneration of living standards in urban areas.

The green parties, which first gained power in West German local authorities and then in the national Parliament, have on the whole been able to broaden their electoral appeal by leaving behind, at least on a public level, most of the extreme-left factions which contributed to their formation in the late 1970s. Once in office they have proved to be very shrewd political operators, extracting compromises from both social democratic and centre-right parties wherever they have been able to make their political weight felt. In fact, there are few of the major political parties in Europe which have not adopted some of their demands.

European communist parties appear, on the whole, to have fared badly from the damaging clashes in the late 1970s and early 1980s between the orthodox pro-Soviet factions and the relatively non-doctrinaire 'Eurocommunist' parties. Of the former type, the French Communist Party (PCF) has seen its electoral support drop most steeply, obtaining only 9.8 per cent of the national vote in the 1986 elections, against 16.2 per cent in 1981. In Finland, the bitter split between orthodox communists and Eurocommunists contributed in 1983 to their exclusion from the governing coalition. Only Italy, in fact, has a really flourishing Eurocommunist party, the second strongest in the country.

III   Political systems and political parties

Austria, a federal republic of nine provinces, is governed by a bicameral parliamentary system in which the national council (*Nationalrat*) is the main legislative body. Its 183 members are elected for a four-year term by a system of proportional representation. Typically for a federal system, each of the provinces maintains its own assembly and government.

The onset of economic difficulties has deeply eroded the traditional political consensus in Austria, and in November 1986 the ruling Socialist Party was forced into an uncomfortable coalition with the right-wing Freedom Party. The new government, led as before by Franz Vranitzky as Federal Chancellor, comprises eight ministers from each party and one independent. In 1986 the Socialists held 80 of the parliamentary seats (previously 90), while the Freedom Party had 18 (12), the People's Party 77 (81), and the Greens entered parliament for the first time with eight seats.

Belgium is a constitutional monarchy with a bicameral legislature comprising a 106-member senate and a 212-member chamber of representatives, in which the four-party centre-right coalition of Christian Social and Liberal parties holds 115 seats. Particular importance, however, is attached to the three provincial parliaments in the Dutch-speaking Flemish region, the French-speaking Wallonia and the capital Brussels, where a large majority speak French. Local government powers have been extended to incorporate a considerable degree of fiscal and economic autonomy, in deference to the severe regional conflicts between French and Dutch speakers. Such are the linguistic divisions, in fact, that each of the three major political groupings finds it expedient to separate into two parallel Dutch- and French-speaking parties.

Like Belgium, Denmark is a constitutional monarchy, with a 179-seat unicameral assembly, the *Folketing*. Danish politics have been very finely balanced in the 1980s, with strong opposition to Poul Schlüter's Conservative-led government over such issues as agriculture, taxation and the continued membership of the European Community. An inconclusive election result in 1984 left Schlüter's party, with 42 of the 179 seats, dependent on a broad-based coalition of Liberals, Faeroese, Greenland and Radical Party members, who between them secured a one-seat majority with 90 of the 179 seats.

Finland's president is technically empowered to conduct a wide range of political activities, but in the last two decades these have been limited to the critical area of foreign affairs. He is appointed by an electoral college which is itself elected by popular vote, and he appoints the premier and council of state (government) personally. Finland has a unicameral 200-member legislature in which the Social Democrats, the Centre Party and the Swedish People's Party retained power in the 1983 elections while the conservative National Coalition was removed from the coalition. Finland comprises 12 provinces, each of which has its own governor, and 461 municipalities.

France is the only European country with a fully executive president. Elected directly by universal suffrage for a seven-year term of office, he appoints the prime minister and government in accordance with the results of parliamentary elections. The French political system is notable for the high degree of centralization – a policy which also extends to the country's overseas territories. Since 1982, however, the control of the centre has been reduced by laws extending greater powers to the 22 regions and 96 departments. The bicameral parliament comprises a senate whose 318 members are elected for a nine-year term, a third of them coming up for re-election every three years. The national assembly, the main legislative body, has 491 members including 17 from overseas departments and territories, who are elected every five years.

Apart from the one five-year interval between 1981 and 1986, French politics have traditionally been dominated by parties of the right wing, the Gaullist *Rassemblement pour la République* and the *Union pour la Démocratie Française*. Sure enough, it was a coalition of these two, with a slim parliamentary majority, which resumed power when the socialists (212 seats, and still the largest single party) lost power. Initially, however, the right-wing government of Jacques Chirac (RPR) has had to work under the socialist President Mitterrand – a so-called 'cohabitation' which was still proving tricky in 1987.

The Federal Republic of Germany comprises eight regions (*Länder*), two city states (Hamburg and Bremen) and, for all practical purposes, West Berlin – although the latter is technically under the joint control of the post-war occupying powers, the USA, France, the UK and the Soviet Union. The main legislative body is the *Bundestag* (federal assembly), based in Bonn, half of whose 498 voting members are elected by a system of constituency lists and half by straightforward proportional representation. Any party must obtain at least 5 per cent of the national/regional vote to gain representation in the *Bundestag* or any of the powerful *Land* assemblies. The *Bundestag* also includes 22 directly-appointed West Berlin deputies, who may be consulted but who have no vote. The *Bundesrat* (upper house) too has four non-voting delegates from West Berlin in addition to the 41 members delegated by the *Land* governments.

Elections to the *Bundestag* were held in January 1987, when the Social Democrats won 186 seats (down from 193 in 1983, but still the biggest party) and the ruling Christian Democratic Union obtained 174 (191), while its Bavarian coalition partner, the Christian Social Union, won 49 (53). The liberal Free Democrats raised their standing from 34 seats to 46, and the Greens from 27 seats to 42.

The Greek constitution, introduced in 1975, established a 300-seat unicameral assembly which has been governed since 1981 by the communist-oriented Panhellenic Socialist Movement (Pasok) of Dr Andreas Papandreou, with 172 seats. Pasok has, however, been losing electoral support in recent years as its tough austerity programme, introduced as an antidote to earlier excessive spending, has started to bite. The main opposition comes from the centre-right New Democracy Party, which ruled from 1975 to 1981.

The Republic of Ireland vests its legislative power in a bicameral assembly, comprising the 166-member *Dail Eireann* (lower house) and the 60-member *Seaned Eireann* (upper house). The office of president of the republic is largely ceremonial. Led by the *Taoiseach* (prime minister), deputies to the *Dail* are elected for five-year terms, according to a complex system of single transferable votes in multi-seat constituencies. In the March 1987 elections *Fianna Fail*, led by Charles Haughey, obtained 81 seats, while the former prime minister Garret Fitzgerald's party *Fine Gael* obtained 51, the Progressive Democrats won 14, Labour obtained 12, the Workers' Party four and independents four.

Italy's 1948 constitution created a bicameral parliament comprising the 630-member chamber of deputies, directly elected by universal adult suffrage, and the 315-member senate, whose members are appointed by the numerous regional assemblies. Italian politics have always been very volatile, with few post-war governments lasting as long as twelve months. The scene has traditionally been dominated by the two major parties, the Christian Democrats, who obtained 225 seats in the 1983 elections, and the communist PCI, which achieved 198 seats. The Italian Socialist Party, with 73 seats, found itself holding the balance of power in 1983–1987 and achieved an unusual three-year period of stability under Bettino Craxi before falling victim once again to the bitter infighting which has characterized the traditionally unwieldy coalitions in Italy. Other important parties include the neo-fascist MSI (41 seats in 1983) and the Republicans (29 seats).

The Grand Duchy of Luxembourg is governed by a unicameral chamber of deputies whose membership was increased in 1984 to 64 members. In the elections of that year the governing coalition of the Christian Social Party and the Democratic Party was returned, with 25 seats and 14 seats respectively; the Socialists, however, raised their strength by half to 21 seats, while the Greens entered the chamber for the first time.

The Netherlands is a constitutional monarchy governed by a bicameral parliament comprising an upper house of 75 members and a second chamber whose 150 members are elected for a four-year term of office. General elections held in May 1986 to the second chamber showed a clear convergence of opinion behind the ruling Christian Social/Liberal coalition and away from the dozens of fringe parties and splinter groups which have complicated Dutch politics in recent decades. Prime Minister Ruud Lubbers' Christian Social Party obtained 54 seats (up from 45 in 1982), while support for the Liberals fell from 36 to 27 seats; meanwhile, however, the socialist vote also solidified behind Labour (up from 36 seats to 52).

Norway, a constitutional monarchy, is governed by the *Storting*, a 157-member unicameral assembly to which the state council (government) answers. In the early 1980s the idea of abolishing the monarchy surfaced, but the proposal to proclaim a republic was finally quashed in 1983 by a vote in the *Storting*.

Elections in September 1985 produced an unhappily indecisive result, in view of the tough action needed to rectify the numerous shortcomings in the economy. Although Kaare Willoch's Conservative-led coalition remained in power, it was left with only 80 of the 157 seats, while the opposition Socialists, Liberals and Left Socialists increased their hold from 72 seats to 77. The fragile coalition collapsed in April 1986 after losing a vote of confidence on an economic austerity package by one vote, and shortly afterwards Mrs Gro Harlem Brundtland was called in to head a minority Labour government. Brundtland thereupon announced an immediate 12 per cent devaluation of the krone and drastic austerity measures – much as her predecessor was in fact planning to do.

Portugal's 1976 constitution vests legislative authority in a 250-member legislative assembly, elected by popular vote, which draws on the council of state for advice. The president is directly elected for a five-year term, and he then appoints the prime minister; since 1982, his powers have been diminishing as the democratic structure gains in solidity. Elections held in July 1987 confirmed the dominance of premier Anibal Cavaco Silva and of his Social Democratic Party, which raised its share of the vote to 52 per cent, from only 24 per cent in 1983, and which secured 146 of the 250 seats in parliament. The Socialist Party (PSP) of the President and former premier Mario Soares dropped to 22 per cent of the vote, while the right-wing Democratic Renewal Party (PRD) of the country's former military leader, Gen. Antonio Eanes, suffered a stunning defeat with less than 5 per cent of the vote – compared with 18 per cent in 1983.

Spain, a constitutional monarchy, has been holding free elections since 1975. The *Cortes* (parliament) is a bicameral system comprising a 350-member congress of deputies and a senate (both elected by popular vote for four-year terms of office). Spanish politics in the mid-1980s have been marked by uncertainties in the centre of the political spectrum, which have allowed the ruling Socialist Party of Felipe Gonzalez Marquez to make the best of its declining support. Capitalizing on such recent successes as Spain's entry to the EEC and its reaffirmation of NATO, Gonzalez called elections in June 1986, in which his party won 184 seats (compared with 202 in 1982), while the Popular Coalition (the main opposition grouping) stagnated at 105. Meanwhile, the Democratic and Social Centre Party (CDS) raised itself from 2 to 19 seats, and the Convergence and Union Party (CiU) went up from 12 to 18 seats. Regional devolution of administrative powers has been under way since 1978, and in 1980–1983 regional elections to local bodies were held for the first time in various parts of the country.

Sweden is a constitutional monarchy in which the unicameral parliament, the 349-member *Riksdag*, is elected for the relatively short term of three years in office. National referenda may also be held for guidance on major issues, but they cannot be used for legislative purposes.

Elections held in September 1985 left the ruling Social Democrats dependent on the Communist Party for their working majority in parliament, with only 159 seats (compared with 166 in 1982). The Communists held 19 seats, while the centre-right opposition vote shifted from the Conservative Party (down from 86 to 76) and the Centre Party (down from 56 seats to 44), toward the Liberals (up from 21 seats to 51). Following the assassination in February 1986 of Premier Olof Palme, Ingvar Carlsson was inaugurated as Prime Minister in March 1986, at the head of a socialist government.

The Swiss Confederation comprises 26 cantons and half-cantons, which are governed by a bicameral assembly. The *Nationalrat* (lower house) comprises 200 members, elected for a four-year term, and a 46-member council of states representing the cantons. The *Bundesrat* (cabinet) is elected for four years by both chambers of parliament, with the office of president (prime minister) and vice-president rotating annually. The 1983 elections gave the Radical Democrats 54 seats in the national council, the Social Democrats 47, the Christian Democrats 42 and the Centre Democrats 23.

The ruling four-party coalition is a broad-based amalgam of centre-right, liberal and social democratic interests, and its composition, like that of the cabinet, has remained unchanged in party terms since 1959. An uncharacteristic dispute did break out in 1984, however, in which the Social Democrats came close to leaving the coalition when the parliament rejected its nomination of a woman for a ministerial position. (Another woman, Dr Elisabeth Kopp, was, however, accepted the following year.) Switzerland makes frequent use of national referenda to decide key issues, presenting batches of issues to the national and cantonal electorates about twice a year.

The United Kingdom, a parliamentary monarchy, is the only major European country to have no formal constitution, relying instead on the body of law. Legislative power is vested in the bicameral legislature comprising the 650-member House of Commons (elected for a five-year term of office) and the House of Lords, an important consultative body of hereditary and appointed representatives.

British politics have been dominated since 1977 by the Conservative Party led by Prime Minister Margaret Thatcher, which was returned to power for a third term of office in elections held during June 1987. The Conservatives gained 374 of the 650 seats in the House of Commons, compared with 395 in the 1983 elections, while Labour won 227 seats, up from 207 in 1983, the Liberal Party representation was unchanged at 17 seats and the Social Democratic Party (essentially a breakaway group from the Labour Party) obtained five seats, one less than in 1983. Two Northern Ireland parties, the Official Unionists and the Ulster Unionists, are also represented in the Commons.

Unlike most other European countries, Britain does not use any form of proportional representation in national elections, preferring the first-past-the-post system in which only the candidate obtaining most votes in a particular constituency can be elected. The system inevitably favours larger parties to the virtual exclusion of smaller ones and fringe groups; the absence of party lists also means that by-elections must be held whenever seats are vacated in mid-term.

IV   Current situation/key issues

Conflicts of interest between Western Europe and the United States have taken many forms in recent years. During the early 1980s, Washington has in fact declared many European policies to be against its own national interests, and it has periodically sought to apply counter-measures against Europe – while at the same time attempting, as in the wake of the Polish crisis of 1981, to force European companies to act in accordance with US law (see Chapter 2). Further political strains have developed from the nagging suspicion in some countries, notably Denmark, that Washington might regard Western Europe as a military buffer zone, rather than as a solid bulwark against any Soviet aggression.

Political solidarity and co-operation between European nations are also desirable for more practical considerations. The mounting cost of technical research on a range of advanced scientific and industrial projects has made it advantageous to pool both manufacturing resources and technological know-how. Political cohesion has also helped to promote essential standardization in various fields; largely through the agency of the European Community, which links 12 of the more important countries, talks have started on the harmonization of transport links, telecommunications standards and (gradually) customs unions.

In the financial field, the mid-1980s have seen renewed efforts to harmonize financial services, company legislation and stock market practices – none of which could be accomplished without the renewed cultivation of both bilateral and multilateral links which have become commonplace in this decade. As Chapter 2 has already noted, the various treaties between the EEC and the European Free Trade Association have extended the scope for co-operation well beyond the Community itself.

There is, however, still deep disagreement on a wide range of issues. Transnational considerations such as the safety of nuclear power (especially in the wake of the 1986 Chernobyl disaster), the siting of new nuclear reactors close to national borders and the dumping of nuclear waste at sea have all aroused fierce controversy and occasional hostility between neighbouring states. Chemical pollution of rivers such as the Rhine has for many years been a bone of contention between France and West Germany, which has accused Paris of dumping industrial waste into the river on the stretch where it borders the two countries. In 1986 a fire at Switzerland's Sandoz plant released enough chemicals into the river's source to destroy much of its wildlife along several hundred kilometres of the river inside Germany.

There is also agitation in West Germany and in Scandanavian countries about the issue of acid rain, and this has been accompanied by pressure on other countries to reduce their own levels of atmospheric pollution. The problem has not gained wide appreciation in the United Kingdom, one of the major sources of the sulphur compounds in question, whose government still resists legislation to curb these emissions, while also querying the other countries' findings that they are in fact to blame for the clouds of dilute sulphuric acid vapour which devastate forest regions. Acid rain has been especially serious in West Germany's Black Forest, where it is estimated to have killed half the trees since the early 1970s.

The swing to the right in many European countries has been accompanied by attempts both to rationalize state industries and to reduce government subsidies to the industrial sector wherever it can be done without endangering research. The issues of steel and shipbuilding are examined in Chapter 2; but for many governments the rising level of interest in international stock markets has provided tantalizing short-term alternatives.

By selling off state assets such as nationalized industries, especially the profit-making ones, to the private sector, governments have been able to kill several birds with one stone. Firstly, these sales help to protect the state against potential liabilities; secondly, they bring in a much-needed one-off boost to the governments' cash-flows; and thirdly, they may be presented as encouraging free enterprise and competition (as, for example, in the 1985 privatization of British Telecom or the 1986–1987 sales of state industrial and banking assets in France). Finally, by accommodating the booming world demand for securities, they have so far given national stock markets a major boost, which in turn has lent them credibility in the international equity business.

Even socialist governments have been obliged in the mid-1980s to acknowledge the advantages of privatizing nationalized industries. While the British Labour Party remains bitterly opposed to the idea, its French counterpart was actively preparing a range of sell-offs while it was in power. In Portugal, Austria, Italy and Spain, too, privatizations have been in the air, under socialist auspices.

Unemployment remains an almost universal and practically insoluble problem in the late 1980s, and despite exchanges of ideas within the EEC there is little co-ordination of attempts to limit its impact. Better progress is being achieved on the security front, where a spate of international terrorist activity and an increasing penetration of European countries by drug dealers have combined to encourage much tighter joint surveillance of the international movements of suspects. By 1987, however, progress on the improvement of extradition procedures was still slow.

The division of Berlin, a political island far away in the middle of East Germany, remains a difficult subject in the later 1980s, not only for West Germany but for the four post-war occupying powers. Under the 1971 four-power agreement neither half of the former German capital may be formally incorporated into either the Federal Republic or the German Democratic Republic; in practice, however, Bonn has been busily strengthening its political and economic links with West Berlin in the 1980s, and these days the Soviet Union receives not much more than perfunctory condemnation for claiming that Berlin (by which it means East Berlin) is the capital of the GDR. But the Berlin Wall, which was built literally overnight by East Germany in 1961, remains a stark reminder that the issue is still unsettled, and East Germany keeps up the pressure on the West with periodic intensive border checks on passenger vehicles, whose effect is practically to bring the transit motorways to West Germany to a halt.

Security problems in Northern Ireland have remained a daily issue for the British Government in the mid-1980s, with periodic and sustained campaigns of violence being conducted both by pro-Irish Catholic factions and (especially recently) by militants in the Protestant majority. Special outrage has been expressed by Protestants at the Anglo-Irish Agreement of November 1985, which provided for an Intergovernmental Conference of UK and Irish officials to cope with legal, political and security matters of common interest, and to promote cross-border co-operation.

The Agreement gives Ireland a mechanism through which it can make proposals on certain bodies appointed by the British Northern Ireland Secretary. But while well received internationally, the opposition voiced by Northern Ireland's Official Unionists and Democratic Unionists, and by *Sinn Fein* in Northern Ireland, has been augmented by that from Ireland's *Fianna Fail*, which came to power in Dublin in the 1987 elections; consequently, its prospects in 1987 seem less than ideal.

Switzerland remains the only major European country in 1987 to stay a non-member of the United Nations. Its government failed in March 1986 to gain approval for the idea of membership when it put it to a referendum. Switzerland is, however, the headquarters of the UN Economic Commission for Europe, stationed at the Palais des Nations in Geneva.

In south-eastern Europe, Greece and Turkey have remained at loggerheads over a range of issues – most notably the status of Cyprus and the territorial rights attaching to the seabed in the Aegean Sea which separates them. Cyprus, whose population is about one-quarter Turkish-speaking, has been effectively divided in two since 1974, when Turkish troops occupied the northern half of the island in protest at what they saw as Greek Cypriot oppression of their fellows; later, the Turkish Cypriots established the so-called Turkish Federated State of Northern Cyprus, and despite strenuous efforts by the United Nations Secretary-General to reach an agreement on some kind of bi-zonal federated state, the Greek Cypriots have so far shown no interest in the direct negotiations being urged by the Turkish speakers.

The Aegean seabed issue is a unique case in international law. Under the usual conventions on continental shelves, the seabed between two countries like Greece and Turkey would be split down the middle, as logic would suggest. But Greece owns most of the islands in the Aegean, up to within a few miles of the Turkish coast; by claiming a twelve-mile territorial limit around each one, it is effectively laying claim to all the viable shipping passages, and it could thus cut off northern Turkey's ports, as well as the entrance to the Black Sea, at will. So far, most of the open confrontations over the issue have revolved around oil prospecting rights, but clashes over military movements in both sea and air space have been frequent as well.

V European defence

Western Europe's long-term defence strategy has been the subject of much debate since the late 1970s, and despite some convergence of opinion in the mid-1980s it was clear by the start of 1987 that the topic would remain a source of controversy for some time to come. The principal forum for debate has so far been the North Atlantic Treaty Organization (NATO), the military grouping formed in 1949 which links all West European nations except Austria, Finland, Ireland, Sweden and Switzerland with the armed forces of the United States and Canada. (France is something of a nominal NATO member, having withdrawn in 1966 from the integrated structure of the alliance, in favour of its own forces.)

For all effective purposes, the strategic threat to Western Europe is generally agreed to be from the Soviet Union and its East European allies, and NATO strategy is accordingly geared to the defence of Europe against such an attack. NATO members (except France) each place part of their military resources at the disposal of the organization, and they engage in joint military manoeuvres analagous to those of the Warsaw Pact armed forces. There is a heavy concentration of NATO ground forces in West Germany, perceived as the logical through-route for a ground-based invasion from the east. Long- and medium-range intelligence operations are conducted in Norway, West Germany, Greece and northern Turkey, and further support derives from satellites and other equipment.

The last 15 years have seen a major build-up of tactical nuclear weapons within the Warsaw Pact, and in 1987 it was apparent that its stocks of both missiles and warheads greatly exceeded the combined strengths of NATO's missiles and the separately-maintained nuclear deterrents of Britain and France. The Soviet Union has so far refused to allow Western inspectors to verify its adherence to such arms limitation agreements as the (now defunct) SALT and SALT II talks with the USA, and the problem of assessing strengths has been further complicated by the development of multi-warhead missiles, rockets capable of carrying either nuclear or conventional explosive payloads, and mobile launchers. NATO and the Warsaw Pact do, however, undertake to warn one another in advance of any conventional military manoeuvres they might be planning, and this mechanism has worked well in the past.

In the 1980s, the mainspring of NATO's strategic defence policy, and also the main source of conflict between its members, has been the December 1979 decision to adopt the so-called 'twin-track' approach to nuclear weapons systems. On the one hand, the NATO partners agreed to press the Soviet Union for negotiations with the United States on the reduction of long-range nuclear missiles, while also making fresh proposals to the ongoing long-term Mutual Balanced Force Reduction (MBFR) talks in Geneva. On the other hand, NATO undertook to replace most of its existing ground-launched Pershing I-A long-range missiles with 108 of the new generation of Pershing II-A missiles, sited mainly in West Germany, and with 464 of its mobile ground-launched cruise missiles in West Germany, the United Kingdom, Belgium and the Netherlands.

By the mid-1980s the Soviet Union was insisting that talks on missiles should be linked to the abandonment of the United States' Strategic Defence Initiative – the so-called 'Star Wars' project involving US satellites capable of pre-emptive action against Soviet missiles while in flight. In early 1987, however, it appeared that the two issues had been recognized as separate and that progress towards verification of any proposed treaty was also being achieved.

Although each of the sovereign states of Western Europe maintains its own armed forces, and although the non-members Austria, Sweden and Switzerland have declared themselves neutral in military terms, there is relatively little doubt that each of them ultimately relies to some extent on NATO's protection. It is also reasonable to say that NATO would be hard pressed to make an effective defence of Western Europe without at least their tacit co-operation in the event of a ground-level invasion by the Soviet bloc.

Sweden has so far been the country most sorely tried by its independent military status. Three times between 1980 and 1982, Stockholm protested to the Soviet Union over the presence of Soviet submarines within its territorial waters; in 1981, indeed, the Russian vessel became firmly wedged on the rocks and had to be floated off by Swedish engineers, amid fierce Soviet denials that the radioactivity they detected in its missile tubes came from nuclear warheads. Only months earlier, by an embarrassing coincidence, the Soviet President Leonid Brezhnev had renewed his calls for making the Baltic a nuclear-free zone.

VI Future developments

In 1987 it seems practically certain that political co-operation in

Western Europe will continue to develop, as the external trade pressures persist and the need for harmonization of industrial and especially financial activities becomes more intense. As a result, the crucial role of the European Community and its close relationship with the European Free Trade Association will remain a focus of political and economic co-operation. It is still possible, however, that Denmark may follow Greenland out of the Community to pursue its Scandinavian interests more closely.

The political drift to the right, caused by economic recession in the early 1980s, may be expected to reverse toward the end of the decade as increasing levels of affluence turn the electorate's attention back toward social issues. There will, however, be only a slow reduction of unemployment levels (except perhaps in Spain), and diverging standards of living in Belgium, the Netherlands, the UK, Greece and Italy are likely to exacerbate existing social tensions.

There is no immediate prospect of any severe curtailments of political rights in Europe, even in Turkey where military coups have happened three times in a generation. In Spain, it appears that the last of the Francoist uprisings petered out in 1986.

The trend toward privatization of nationalized industries will continue, and will gain fresh impetus from the development of round-the-clock international securities dealing and the deregulation of financial services. It should be possible for EEC members (but by no means all Scandinavian countries) to harmonize stock exchange regulations by 1992.

The Berlin issue is, in a sense, dormant in 1987; the local economy is doing better with both political and economic assistance from Bonn, and the conflicting claims of East and West Germany are being quietly passed over by both sides. But, by the same token, there is unlikely to be sufficient political will to stand a confrontation over the issue in the late 1980s; both sides have been cultivating goodwill, and there is too much to lose.

The Northern Ireland Agreement between Britain and the Irish Republic will prove hard to implement, given the opposition of the ruling *Fianna Fail* in Dublin, but its provisions will remain in force. Neither country is prepared to let up in its effort against terrorism, and political tensions in Northern Ireland are likely to rise as the economic climate worsens.

The Greek/Turkish disputes over Cyprus and the Aegean are

unlikely to find full resolution, and this will continue to trouble NATO in its efforts to co-ordinate Western defence policies. Pressure from the USA, which effectively controls the flow of military aid to these countries, will, however, exert a calming influence. Meanwhile, the US-Soviet arms talks in Geneva will continue to make progress – although it is far from clear how the proposed verification measures could work.

CHAPTER FOUR
PAN-EUROPEAN ECONOMIC TRENDS

I Economic growth

Despite a slump in the second half of 1986, the economic upswing in West Europe has now lasted for roughly four years. The absence of any periods of vibrant growth in output, however, have persisted since the 1970s. The region recently began to fall behind other industrialized areas as a result. Between 1982 (the last year of the previous recession) and 1986, growth in total real output of West Europe was roughly 9 per cent. This compares with a 16 per cent increase in the USA.

The data in Table 4.1 (p56) show that GDP in Western Europe grew at 2.5 per cent in 1985 and 1986 and at a even slower pace in previous years. The smaller economies have generally tended to perform better than the larger ones. Austria, Denmark, Norway, Portugal and Switzerland all recorded increases in economic activity of 3 per cent or more in 1985. Expansion of output has received much of its support from external demand as the growth of exports exceeded that of imports. On the domestic side, investment in machinery and equipment and private consumption also contributed to growth of real output.

A closer look at the long-term changes in several components of aggregate demand is given in Table 4.2 (p56). Private consumption naturally accounts for the greatest portion of aggregate demand. Over the last twenty years, the share of this component in GDP has generally remained stable, declining only in several of the smaller economies (Denmark, Finland, Ireland, Norway and Sweden). In recent years, however, movements in private consumption have departed from the long-term trend. Although the pace of growth accelerated moderately in 1985 – mainly in response to the fall in

TABLE 4.1   GROWTH OF GROSS DOMESTIC PRODUCT IN WEST EUROPE[a]
(annual percentage change)

Country[b]	1983	1984	1985	1986
West Germany	1.5	2.7	2.6	2.5
France	0.7	1.5	1.1	2.3
United Kingdom	3.8	2.2	3.7	2.5
Italy	−0.2	2.8	2.3	2.8
Spain	1.8	1.9	2.2	3.0
Netherlands	1.4	2.4	1.7	1.5
Sweden	2.4	4.0	2.2	1.7
Switzerland	0.7	2.1	4.0	2.6
Belgium	−0.3	1.7	1.5	1.6
Austria	2.1	2.0	3.0	2.0
Norway	4.5	5.6	4.2	3.8
Denmark	2.0	3.4	3.8	3.3
Finland	2.9	2.8	2.8	2.0
Greece	0.4	2.8	2.1	0.4
Portugal	−0.3	−1.6	3.3	3.7
Ireland	1.9	4.2	2.0	0.5
Total	1.6	2.4	2.5	2.5

Source: ECE, OECD
[a] Calculated at 1980 market prices and exchange rates
[b] Countries are ranked by level of GDP in 1985

interest rates – rates of increase have been below historical levels since 1983.

Table 4.2 shows a substantial increase in the share of government consumption since 1965. For the region as a whole, the unweighted average was 14 per cent in 1965 but had climbed to 19 per cent by 1984. Like private consumption, recent trends in this demand component have departed from the long-term trend. Government consumption grew by only 3 per cent in the combined period 1984–85. That pace, which was less than growth of total domestic demand in most West European countries, reflects the cutbacks on public expenditures which governments have introduced as part of their anti-inflationary programmes.

The share of a third major component of aggregate demand, gross domestic capital formation, has declined during the past twenty years. On average, European expenditures in this category were equivalent to roughly one-fourth of GDP in 1965 but had fallen to one-fifth of the total in 1984. Movements in recent years show some acceleration as investment has been bolstered by the gradual economic recovery. The modest improvement, however, conceals

TABLE 4.2 COMPONENTS OF AGGREGATE DEMAND IN WEST
EUROPEAN COUNTRIES[a] 1965 AND 1985
(as a percentage of real GDP)

	Government final consumption		Private consumption		Gross fixed capital investment	
	1965	1985	1965	1985	1965	1985
Austria	13	19	59	56	28	23
Belgium[b]	13	17	64	66	23	15
Denmark[b]	16	25	59	54	26	19
Finland	14	20	60	55	28	24
France	13	16	61	66	25	13
Greece	12	20	73	70	26	21
Ireland[b]	14	19	72	58	24	22
Italy	15	19	62	63	20	18
Netherlands[b]	15	16	59	60	27	18
Norway[b]	15	19	56	47	30	25
Portugal[b]	12	14	68	70	25	23
Spain[b]	7	14	71	67	25	18
Sweden	18	27	56	49	27	20
Switzerland	10	13	60	62	30	28
United Kingdom	17	21	64	60	20	18
West Germany	15	20	56	55	28	20
Average (unweighted)	14	19	62	60	26	20

Source: World Bank, OECD
[a] Government consumption is composed of all current expenditures by all levels of government. Capital expenditures on defence and security are included in this category. Private consumption is the market value of all purchases by households and non-profit institutions. Gross domestic investment is all outlays for fixed assets plus net changes in inventories. Calculations are based on data at constant prices.
[b] Ending year for data on private consumption and gross fixed capital formation is 1984

wide differences in various types of investment which are discussed later in this chapter.

II Productivity

Growth in labour productivity – both for the entire economy and for the manufacturing sector – has decelerated slightly in Western Europe. The result can be attributed to the fact that expansion of output in preceding years was usually accompanied by falling or stagnating levels of employment. By 1985, the possibilities for boosting output without simultaneously raising employment were limited, particularly in those sectors where demand was relatively buoyant.

While these circumstances help to explain recent movements in labour productivity, there has been a steady reduction in the rate of growth that can be traced back to the early 1960s. In 1961–73, labour productivity in Western Europe grew at a pace exceeding 4 per cent per annum. However, in 1974–79 the annual rate fell to 2.1 per cent and then declined to just over one per cent in 1980–83. By the mid-1980s, the growth of labour productivity was less than one-fourth the level attained in the 1960s. This long-term deceleration in growth of productivity is a feature which is not unique to Western Europe. In fact, corresponding rates for the USA were even lower. The persistant decline nevertheless suggests that factors other than short-term forces are at work.

Although international comparisons of productivity trends are commonly based on estimates of labour productivity, this is not the only method (or even the most appropriate one) for judging progress. An alternative approach takes account of total factor productivity. Use of the latter measure recognizes that gains in labour productivity depend on the efficiency of installed machinery and equipment as well as labour skills. Increases in labour productivity may result from the greater efficiency of workers or they may be the consequence of a relative increase in the availability of capital per worker (i.e. capital-substitution or capital-deepening). When the discussion of productivity is placed in this broader context, current trends depend not only on workforce characteristics but also on the investment climate in earlier years, on rates of capital usage and the efficiency of the capital allocation process.

The combination of economic shocks, imbalances and policy responses which characterized much of the 1970s are known to have created an environment for capital formation which was less favourable than in previous years. The favourable demand conditions which prevailed in the first half of the 1970s created an environment where profit expectations were high. In those circumstances the rate of fixed investment accelerated and led to a rapid exploitation of technical advances. Buoyant demand made an indirect contribution to the growth of productivity: it helped to drive resources out of low productivity areas and to boost overall efficiency. But these conditions were all dramatically reversed at the close of the 1970s. The resultant slowdown in capital formation contributed to the decline in the growth of labour productivity which occurred in 1979–83.

Another reason for the fall in labour productivity has been a parallel drop in capital productivity (output in relation to capital stock). Low levels of output and shrinking demand led to the fall in capital productivity. The result has been a decline in rates of capacity utilization which, by the early 1980s, were significantly below historical levels. When variations in rates of capital utilization were taken into account, estimates of growth in productivity were raised moderately.

A third possible reason for the slow growth of labour productivity is that the means of allocating capital in Western Europe have gradually become less efficient. In order to gauge the efficiency of the capital allocation process, variations in capital intensity must first be identified. If, for example, the degree of capital intensity has fallen in a particular industry, a simultaneous slowdown in labour productivity can be partially attributed to this event. Slow growth of labour skills and/or efficiency would not necessarily be the under-lying cause. After adjusting for changes in capital intensity, studies have shown that changes in capital intensity are found to have depressed the growth of labour productivity in a limited number of countries – among them Austria, Belgium and West Germany.

Table 4.3 (p60) summarizes the results of two exercises to estimate labour productivity and total factor productivity in the manufacturing sector of several West European economies. Although growth of both measures has generally exceeded corresponding rates for the whole economy, the rate of expansion declined noticeably in most countries after 1979. The figures show an acceleration in only three countries – Finland, Sweden and the United Kingdom. More generally, the close relationship between the two sets of estimates would seem to indicate that changes in total factor productivity have frequently been a major reason for the slowdown in growth of labour productivity.

III   Incomes and wages

The movement of income and wages in Western Europe contrasts

TABLE 4.3   PRODUCTIVITY CHANGES IN THE MANUFACTURING
SECTOR
(average annual rates of growth)

	Changes in labour productivity[a]			Changes in total factor productivity[b]		
	1973-83	1973-79	1979-84	1973-83	1973-79	1979-83
Austria	3.6	3.6	3.6	2.4	2.6	2.1
Belgium	5.9[c]	6.5	5.0[c]	4.8	5.3	4.1
Denmark[d]	3.6	4.3	2.5	2.9[e]	3.0[e]	2.5[e]
Finland[d]	4.2	3.7	4.6	2.5[e]	2.1[e]	3.1[e]
France	4.7	5.2	4.2	3.3	3.7	2.6
Italy	3.4	3.3	3.6	2.6	2.6	2.5
Netherlands	4.6[c]	5.4	3.3[c]	3.1	3.7	2.3
Norway	2.2	2.2	2.1	0.6[e]	0.5[e]	0.7[e]
Sweden	3.1	2.7	3.6	1.8[e]	1.6[e]	2.1[c]
United Kingdom	2.0	1.5	2.6	1.4	0.7	2.6
West Germany	3.6	4.3	2.7	2.6	3.2	1.6

Source: ECE
[a] Output per hour worked. For Austria, output per person employed
[b] Takes into account capital and labour inputs where both are weighted by factor
   shares in total cost. Figures have been adjusted for variations in capacity
   utilization
[c] 1973–83
[d] Changes in total factor productivity are not adjusted for capacity utilization
[e] Ending period is 1981

markedly with the experience of the USA. In Europe, there has
been a much stronger upward trend of real wages in manufacturing
and a greater inflexibility in wage behaviour in response to adverse
disturbances (e.g. higher prices or a reduction in the growth of
productivity). To the extent that wage rates have not responded to
such disturbances, producers have an incentive to substitute capital
for labour and unemployment is worsened. Other encumbrances to
the smooth functioning of the European labour market are a
substantial gap between producers' wage costs and employees' net
earnings along with a lack of geographical and occupational
mobility. The net effect of all these factors has been a comparatively
rapid rise in real wages which, at times, have exceeded the growth of
productivity.

Table 4.4 provides data showing recent changes in hourly
earnings and labour productivity. With very few exceptions, the
growth of hourly earnings for the economy as a whole was
significantly less in 1981–85 than in 1973–80. A major reason for the

TABLE 4.4   TRENDS IN HOURLY EARNINGS AND LABOUR PRODUCTIVITY

	Hourly earnings for the economy as a whole			Annual change in labour productivity for the economy as a whole[f] (Percentage change over previous year)			Changes in average hourly earnings in manufacturing[h] (per cent)	
	Index of hourly earnings, 1985 (1980=100)	Growth rate of index						
		1973–80	1981–85	1983	1984	1985[g]	1984	1985
Austria[a]	131.2	8.9	5.3	2.9	1.9	2.5	5.0	6.1
Belgium	132.6	11.4	4.7	0.9	1.2	1.5	5.1	3.6
Denmark	141.1	12.6	6.5	1.7	1.2	0.0	4.7	4.8
Finland[b]	156.0	12.8	8.5	3.2	2.9	2.5	10.1	8.4
France	178.4	16.2	11.5	1.2	2.3	2.0	8.1	6.0
Greece	306.8	24.2	24.3	—	—	—	26.3	19.8
Ireland[b]	177.5	19.0	11.2	2.0	5.8[b]	3.5	10.6	7.2
Italy[c]	207.5	22.1	13.6	-0.3	2.2	2.0	11.6	11.3
Netherlands	120.0	8.3	3.6	3.0	2.2	1.5	1.2	4.9
Norway	154.0	11.8	8.8	3.3	3.1	1.0	8.5	7.9
Portugal[d]	244.1	15.5	18.7	—	—	—	18.1	20.8
Spain	197.3	27.0	13.4	3.1	2.5	1.5	9.4	12.3
Sweden	154.1	13.7	8.9	2.0	2.3	3.0	9.6	7.5
Switzerland[a]	103.0	4.0	-1.2	—	—	—	1.8	3.3
United Kingdom[e]	161.1	16.3	8.8	4.4	1.3	3.0	8.7	9.1
West Germany	121.3	6.8	3.4	2.7	2.5	2.0	2.3	4.5

Source: OECD, ECE and author's calculations

[a] Wage data refer to monthly earnings. Manufacturing includes mining
[b] Includes construction and mining
[c] Contractual wages
[d] Daily earnings
[e] Weekly earnings
[f] Real GDP per person employed
[g] Preliminary
[h] The weighted average for all countries with available data was 7.3 per cent in 1984 and 7.5 per cent in 1985

moderate growth in labour costs has been the high levels of unemployment rather than any fundamental change in the way the labour market is functioning. Furthermore, the overall downward trend conceals rises in the labour costs of several countries. Hourly earnings rose three fold in Greece between 1980 and 1985 and doubled in Italy, Portugal and Spain.

When attention is focused on manufacturing, a somewhat different earnings pattern emerges. The weighted average for all countries listed in Table 4.4 shows little change between 1984 and 1985. Again, the variation among countries was a wide one. The growth of earnings stabilized in Denmark and Italy and tended to accelerate only in the United Kingdom and in low-inflation countries (Austria, Netherlands, Switzerland and West Germany). Elsewhere, rates of increases have slowed. The fragmentary evidence on productivity growth in manufacturing (not shown) suggests a trend opposite to that for earnings. A pronounced decline appears to have occurred in Denmark, the Netherlands and Sweden for example. In other countries – particularly France, Italy and the United Kingdom – year-to-year comparisons of productivity growth in manufacturing are somewhat distorted by sizeable reductions in the workforce.

With regard to non-wage sources of income, Table 4.5 shows movements in gross profit shares in the 1980s. Before-tax profits rose briskly in most countries in 1983 and 1984 in response to weakening prices of raw materials and rising consumer demand. Growth vanished in 1985, however, when shares stabilized around their levels in previous years. In that year, profit shares in three countries – the Netherlands, the United Kingdom and West Germany – were still below levels in 1970. In all other countries, however, the 1985 estimates exceeded the corresponding figures for 1980.

IV Investment

In comparison with other industrialized regions, investment in Western Europe has remained sluggish throughout the 1980s. The 1970s had been plagued by a series of economic shocks, imbalances and policy responses which weakened the investment climate. Once economic growth resumed in 1983, the pace of business investment

TABLE 4.5   INDICES OF GROSS PROFIT SHARES IN MANUFACTURING (1970=100)

	1980	1981	1982	1983	1984	1985
Denmark	99.6	98.5	100.4	123.9	125.8	123
Finland[a]	98.3	90.2	88.4	102.1	111.2	102
Ireland[b]	106.3	101.9	103.3	97.6	107.4	110
Netherlands	45.1	26.3	47.0	48.1	71.8	61
Norway[c]	100.0	79.5	72.7	89.3	104.9	111
Sweden	78.8	72.7	86.0	110.2	118.2	114
United Kingdom	71.4	73.9	83.2	90.4	96.8	94
West Germany	80.0	77.0	80.0	86.0	88.8	88

Source: ECE
[a] Net share
[b] Industry
[c] 1980=100

accelerated. But the same was not true for public investment. Along with investment in industrial buildings and housing, public investment in West Europe has remained weak throughout the recovery.

The recovery of fixed investment can be attributed to moderate increases in demand, higher rates of capacity utilization, improved profitability and the desire to increase capacity. Table 4.6 shows that gross fixed investment in 1985 rose in Austria, Finland, Sweden, Switzerland and West Germany. At the same time, the acceleration which began in 1984 in Denmark, Ireland, Italy and the Netherlands continued. However, the slump in gross fixed investment continues in several of the smaller European countries. In Greece, for example, 1985 was the first year since 1979 when fixed investment actually rose. Moreover, this achievement was mainly due to investment by the public sector; fixed investment in the private business sector showed no signs of recovery. In Portugal, fixed investment in 1985 fell for the third consecutive year as a result of a combination of factors including weak output growth, high real rates of interest and cuts in public investment.

Wide variations in the circumstances affecting investment behaviour in these sub-sectors are reflected by the figures in Table 4.6 (p64). Improvements in the climate for business investment in machinery and equipment have been offset by a continued slump of investment in construction and housing. Sluggish investment in construction is mainly due to the limits imposed on public sector investment, while the demand for housing has been depressed by the slow growth of disposable income and interest rates which, by historical standards, are high. The differing effects of investment attitudes has meant that the manufacturing sector has tended to be the major beneficiary of new investment throughout Western Europe. Moreover, it is likely that available figures underestimate the strength of investment in manufacturing. This is so because national accounting practices call for capital assets to be allocated to various sectors on the basis of ownership rather than use. However, an increasing portion of the capital equipment used within the manufacturing sector is leased from other companies, frequently financial firms in the service sector.

TABLE 4.6   ANNUAL CHANGE IN GROSS DOMESTIC FIXED CAPITAL
            FORMATION AND IN MAJOR COMPONENTS
            (percentage change over previous year)

	Real gross domestic fixed capital formation[a]		Investment in machinery and equipment		Structures and buildings	
	1984	1985	1984	1985	1984	1985
Austria	2.0	4.5	4.6	9.0	−0.5	—
Belgium	1.1	3.2	—	—	—	—
Denmark	12.5	8.0	16.0	19.5	9.4	9.4
Finland	−2.0	5.0	1.5	1.1	−4.7	2.0
France	−2.2	0.2	1.5	—	—	—
Greece	−4.7	1.3	—	—	—	—
Ireland	−1.8	2.2	7.0	8.0	−10.0	−4.0
Italy	4.1	4.5	9.5	11.3	−0.5	−1.9
Netherlands	4.3	2.3	8.7	10.5	3.0	−3.0
Norway	11.1	−13.8	16.9	5.1	11.0	−12.0
Portugal	−18.0	−5.0	—	—	—	—
Spain	−3.2	5.0	—	—	—	—
Sweden	3.9	6.3	3.2	16.5	2.0	0.2
Switzerland	4.0	4.7	3.9	9.0	4.1	2.2
United Kingdom	8.2	4.2	6.8[b]	—	9.0	—
West Germany	0.8	−0.8	−0.5	8.8	1.6	−6.7

Source: ECE
[a] The weighted average for percentage change in gross fixed capital formation for all West European countries shown in the table was 1.4 per cent in both 1984 and 1985
[b] Private sector only

Investments in structures and buildings are not subject to the same statistical ambiguities. Imbalances between demand and supply have given rise to acute problems, with repercussions for investment behaviour. Production capacities in the sector sometimes appear to have been excessive owing to the erratic use of government schemes (e.g. in West Germany) which have given temporary boosts to demand for housing followed by severe slumps when the subsidies were removed. For the region as a whole, these imbalances led to a reduction of investment in dwellings during 1981–84 to levels below those in 1975 and substantially less than peak levels achieved in 1980. Altogether, the net effect of opposing movements for investment in machinery and equipment and structures was an increase in total investment in West Europe of 1.4 per cent in both 1984 and 1985.

V   Economic policies: fiscal and monetary

The focus of macroeconomic policy in Western European countries has primarily been geared to achieve medium- rather than short-term objectives. Although unevenly implemented, policies have generally given priority to the goals of restoring financial stability, reducing fiscal deficits and controlling the growth of public spending.

Most countries have tended to accord a somewhat higher priority to the goal of deficit reduction in recent years. However, the ability of governments to make significant cuts in public deficit has been constrained by the exceptionally high rates of unemployment. In the case of the United Kingdom and the Netherlands the fall in world prices for oil and natural gas represented a further complication, while the budget surplus of Norway has been reduced for the same reason. Success has been most apparent among the larger Western European countries. In three of the four largest countries the growth of public expenditures has been curtailed and the central government deficit as a share of GNP has fallen. The only exception is Italy where the central government deficit reached 16 per cent of GNP in 1985 – the largest share in any industrialized country. The situation among the smaller European countries has been somewhat different. In countries other than Denmark and Sweden, deficits have remained unchanged or even risen during the first half of this decade.

Efforts to contain (or reduce) the growth of public expenditure are only one aspect of an overall fiscal strategy. Another important feature concerns the response of the government's revenue system to inflation and the growth of real income. In this sense the fiscal objectives of countries having both low rates of inflation and real growth in income have been more easily realized than for other countries. Because West Germany has enjoyed a combination of low rates of inflation and real growth in income, authorities in that country had more flexibility in their application of policies. They have been able to use their selection of policies to achieve structural as well as fiscal goals. The country has introduced changes in taxes on business incomes, investment credits and other policies intended to change the composition of output. The fiscal restraint sought by British authorities was mainly achieved by boosting revenue, although strenuous efforts to contain the growth of expenditures were also undertaken. In France, a substantial proportion of revenue gains has been obtained through successive increases in social security contributions. This approach, however, was at least temporarily abandoned in 1985 when the government implemented cuts in personal income and business tax. The cuts offset revenue gains derived from increases in social security taxes and other measures. Italy, with a comparatively high rate of inflation, has had to adopt a somewhat different fiscal approach. The steps taken to boost government receipts in 1982 and 1983 proved to have only a temporary effect and the share of this component in GNP levelled off in 1984 and 1985. While attempting to maintain the current level of the tax burden, Italian authorities have begun to stress improved methods of enforcement and measures to prevent the erosion of the tax base.

The European approach is somewhat different in the case of monetary policy. Although the principal objective has been to reduce rates of inflation and inflationary expectations, changes in monetary thinking of many public authorities have now begun to alter the stance of governments. The shift is the result of two major lines of thought with repercussions which extend beyond the conventional boundaries of monetary policy. The first questions the need (or even the desirability) of state regulations of services. In the case of financial services the traditional view was that strict regulation was needed in order to safeguard against fraud, to prevent excessive credit expansion and to control international capital movements. Now that the appeal of these arguments is disputed, major banks and security traders have redoubled their pressure to abolish regulations which may be detrimental to their interests. The second development is the growing impression that unemployment, rather than inflation, is the major problem for macroeconomic policy.

Both trends have tended to undermine the appeal of monetarism. Because European officials (at least those outside the United Kingdom) were particularly uncomfortable with many elements of the monetarist approach, they were quick to distance themselves from it. The standing of monetarism has been further undercut by the fact that such policies relegated much of the responsibility for determination of exchange rates to market forces. The result has been wide swings in real exchange rates which, for reasons noted in Chapter 1, have posed serious problems for Europeans.

As the shift in thinking occurred, governments altered their approaches. The rate of growth in money supply (according to both narrow and broad definitions) during 1985 and 1986 was higher in most Western European countries than in the two preceding years. The acceleration resulted from overshooting target ranges and from modification of these ranges during the target period. Overshooting was a particularly troublesome problem for German authorities as the money stock of the central bank persistently exceeded the target range in 1986. That experience helps to explain the country's reluctance to lower discount rates, despite American pressure. In the United Kingdom, falling oil prices and downward pressure on the pound forced monetary authorities to raise interest rates temporarily in early 1986, only to reverse that process in early 1987. A steady decline of inflation rates in France and West Germany allowed authorities to permit a corresponding drop in nominal rates of interest. In Italy, state sector borrowing exceeded targets for planned borrowing by 13 per cent in 1985. Although the reduced targets for rates of monetary and credit growth were met by the private sector, public sector deficit emerged as a major source of liquidity growth.

VI   Economic outlook

West Europe's feeble economic upswing entered its fourth consecutive year in 1987. Throughout that period, annual growth of output has hovered around 2.5 per cent. A slackening rate of growth in the third and fourth quarters of 1986, coupled with appreciation of European currencies against the dollar, spread doubts about the region's prospects for 1987 and beyond. Prospects over the next several years will depend mainly on developments in the four largest European countries and, particularly, in West Germany. That country's pivotal role is explained not only by the obvious fact that it is the region's largest economy but also because German markets for European exporters will loom more important now that the stimulus of American imports has waned. The outlook for growth in many of the smaller countries is less promising as authorities struggle to overcome government deficits, external imbalances and cyclical problems.

Domestic demand will continue to provide the main growth impetus in most European economies. In this context, the antici-pated growth of private consumption in the next 2–3 years is a major reason for the less than buoyant prospects for overall growth. Domestic demand has constituted the main stimulus to growth in recent years. Private consumption, which is the dominant compo-nent in domestic demand, will continue to play this role in the future. Falling rates of inflation and declining interest rates helped boost private consumption in recent years. However, the effects of these developments on real income have now begun to wane and future increases in private consumption are unlikely to match recent trends.

Future trends in private consumption have implications for private investment. Although investment in manufacturing acceler-ated in recent years, the long-term trend since 1973 remains well below the corresponding rate for 1960–73. Again, this means that overall growth prospects are meagre in comparison with the experience in previous economic upswings. Another implication of recent investment trends is that much of future investment will not provide additions to existing productive capacity but merely serve to offset the scrapping of obsolete capital equipment. Official forecasts for 1987 suggest a modest rise in gross private fixed investment in France, Italy and the United Kingdom. The pace of private investment in West Germany, although generally superior to that of the other large European countries in recent years, is not expected to rise further in the next year. Elsewhere in West Europe, a slowdown in expected growth of total investment is a major reason for dimmer prospects. However, the general restrictive fiscal policies employed in recent years will be continued with depressive effects on investment in the residential and public sectors. In contrast to the expectations for private consumption· and private investment, the outlook for public consumption and investment by the public sector are far less promising, meaning that the bulk of growth in domestic demand will have to depend on the former two components.

With regard to external demand, the trade imbalances of most West European countries have been considerably improved as a result of terms-of-trade gains in recent years. In fact, without such gains the trade balances of several countries would have deteriorated markedly since the volume of imports often rose more rapidly than exports. Any improvement in export performance will largely be due to a recovery in the markets of non-oil developing countries. The outlook, however, is not so bleak in the case of intra-European trade. A slowdown in Germany's net exports seems inevitable owing to the Deutschmark's appreciation against the dollar. At the same time, a number of other European currencies, though appreciating against the dollar, have fallen against the Deutsch mark. The realignment should strengthen external demand and provide a new boost to growth of output. The export prospects of France, Italy, the United Kingdom and other European countries are improved – not only because of stronger demand in West Germany but also as a result of gains in competitiveness due to exchange rate changes. A crucial relationship here will be the link between domestic demand and net exports in the West German economy. If domestic demand in that country proves to be significantly lower than expected, export prospects for the rest of West Europe could be seriously weakened.

The outlook for inflation in West Europe is somewhat brighter. Recent movements of exchange rates, coupled with a decline in prices for intermediates and other industrial inputs have reduced the upward pressure on consumer prices. Future price trends are nevertheless subject to some uncertainty depending on the price of oil and future shifts in exchange rates. Altogether, consumer prices may rise moderately in West Europe although there are strong reasons to expect the underlying rate of cost inflation to remain low.

The short-term prospects for modest growth in employment are also promising. Labour shedding in Europe can be expected to slacken as the earlier moderation of gains in real wages helps to boost profitability. In a limited number of countries an acceleration in growth of output may also contribute to employment gains. Although there are some grounds for optimism about the growth of employment, that trend is unlikely to have any effect on levels of unemployment – particularly without an acceleration in output growth.

The overall policy approach of Western European countries will continue to be growth-accommodating. However, the policy choices available to West Europe's authorities can not be easily disentangled from those of the USA. Any reduction in the US budget deficit would significantly reduce the danger of inflation. European authorities would then have greater freedom of manoeuvre and would be more prone to take short-term steps to ease fiscal policies. A reduction in the US budget deficit would also lead to downward pressure on rates of interest as the fall in net capital imports to the USA frees financial resources for other purposes. The approach adopted by the West German government will be a key element in the region's overall macroeconomic policy in 1987 and 1988. German authorities remain satisfied with the standing policy of fiscal consolidation. In comparison with Japan, Germany's trade links with the USA are modest and the government remains reluctant to relax its fiscal stance despite the significant appreciation of the deutschmark against the US dollar. The present German administration continues to place its hopes on an expansion of domestic demand achieved through tax cuts and reductions in interest rates. It would be prepared to consider an alternative fiscal strategy only if an acceleration in domestic demand fails to materialize.

The ability or willingness of European authorities to boost domestic demand will be crucial over the next few years as this would be necessary in order to offset the region's weaker export position. Because private consumption is unlikely to maintain its present growth momentum, the role of investment becomes especially important. More expansionary fiscal policies will be needed in order to achieve a higher level of fixed investment. In the longer run, the need to bolster the capital formation process – and to improve the efficiency of the system of capital allocation – is essential. Such objectives can be realized only if supported and sustained by policy measures employed for a comparatively long period of time.

CHAPTER FIVE
FINANCE AND BANKING IN EUROPE

I Introduction

Europe offers a wide variety of financial systems in countries with diverse economic and financial backgrounds. The past 30 years have seen a transition from, in general, nationally orientated banks subject to strict exchange control and domestic banking regulations to a more liberal and outward system, with moves in the 1980s in many countries to lower external capital barriers while at the same time increasing competition for domestic transactions. In particular the period has brought the emergence of the Euro-currency markets facilitating international capital raising and external currency deposit-making transactions and the slow development of the financial, banking and monetary aspects of the EEC. Regulation continues to be carried out by national central monetary institutions rather than a single authority for EC member countries although there is a limited amount of international supervision carried out under the direction of the Bank of International Settlements. A European monetary system has been established with a reference currency, the ecu, but the harmonization of banking regulations and the abolition of capital controls between member countries is still to be achieved. Progress so far towards integration of banking systems has to a large extent occurred through market forces, banks and security houses operating a global market strategy, thereby helping to start the move to the removal of capital controls and altering the international monetary policy which characterized the 1960s and 1970s. This in the mid-1980s had started to permeate domestic banking and capital market structures and regulations in several European countries with significant reforms introduced in 1985–87 to improve competition between banks, to increase investor protection and strengthen banks' capital ratios. This is resulting in major changes to the relationship between European banks and financial services companies and is leading in some countries to the development of more widely based banking groups than before.

II European banking and financial services

Banking systems vary considerably between individual European countries and in the mid-1980s were in a state of flux following the moves towards the de-regulation of many domestic financial markets, the globalization of international financial markets and the growth of wider based banking and financial services groups. While some countries, such as Germany and Austria, have traditionally adopted a system of universal banks (where generally no limitations are placed on the type of transactions and activities pursued by the bank and on the maturity structure of assets and liabilities, resulting in services from personal business through to long-term specialist corporate and capital market work being carried out), others such as in the UK and Italy have tended to have a series of individual banks catering for market sectors. On a world scale the overall ranking of European banks declined significantly during the 1970s and 1980s, principally reflecting the growth of Japanese banks and the appreciation of the Japanese yen. Four of the five largest European banks (Table 5.1) are French, the Crédit Agricole in 1980 having been the largest world bank in terms of assets, while eight of the largest 30 European banks are German. In general, the top Austrian, Belgian, French, German, Dutch, Swedish and Swiss banks improved their international positions in the 1970s only to drop rankings in the early 1980s; British and Danish banks lost ground in the 1970s but gained in the early 1980s; and Italian banks saw a declining position throughout this period. In 1986 the top Austrian, Greek, Danish, Eire, Finnish, Luxembourg, Norwegian, Portuguese, Spanish and Swedish banks were respectively numbers 97, 139, 157, 195, 140, 138, 277, 251, 100 and 102 in world ranking.

In Germany at the end of 1986 there were 4,662 banks with 39,979 branches, the size of the branch network having more than trebled over the previous 30 years. The banking system is basically universal with a very low level of concentration (the biggest six commercial

TABLE 5.1   WORLD RANKINGS OF TOP THIRTY EUROPEAN BANKS
(by assets)

Bank	Country	1970	1980	1985	1986
Banque Nationale de Paris	France	15	4	7	6
Crédit Agricole	France	n/a	1	9	8
Crédit Lyonnais	France	21	6	10	10
National Westminster	UK	7	11	14	12
Société Générale	France	34	7	11	14
Deutsche Bank	Germany	24	5	18	15
Barclays Bank	UK	4	9	12	16
Midland Bank	UK	20	26	20	20
Dresdner Bank	Germany	37	8	32	25
Cie Financière de Paribas	France	95	50	31	29
Union Bank of Switzerland	Switzerland	46	31	36	33
Lloyds Bank	UK	33	37	35	35
Swiss Bank Corporation	Switzerland	52	28	41	37
Westdeutsche Landesbank Girozentrale	Germany	14	13	43	38
Banca Nazionale del Lavoro	Italy	9	23	42	39
Commerzbank	Germany	51	15	54	42
Bayerische Vereinsbank	Germany	90	21	52	45
Algemene Bank Nederland	Netherlands	63	33	48	48
Amsterdam-Rotterdam Bank	Netherlands	68	27	58	50
Rabobank	Netherlands	n/a	25	57	55
Banca Commerciale Italiana	Italy	25	38	51	56
Bay. Hypotheken und Wechsel Bank	Germany	73	32	63	57
Istituto Bancario San Paolo di Torino	Italy	71	70	59	59
Crédit Suisse	Switzerland	56	46	65	61
Bayerische Landesbank Giro	Germany	n/a	30	64	62
Deutsche Genossenschaftsbank	Germany	n/a	48	82	63
Standard Chartered Bank	UK	43	59	50	64
Générale de Banque	Belgium	66	45	69	65
Monte dei Paschi di Siena	Italy	45	64	70	66
Cariplo	Italy	31	56	66	67

n/a: not available
Note: Rankings are based on asset size expressed in US dollars at balance sheet dates.
Source: *The Banker*

banks only account for 8.4 per cent of total bank assets) with three main types of bank: commercial banks (308), savings banks (589) and credit co-operatives (3,597). Commercial banks accounted at the end of February 1987 for 23.1 per cent of total banking assets and are engaged in a wide range of deposit, bond, lending and foreign trade activities; savings banks, with 21.7 per cent of total assets, are mainly owned by local authorities and lend to the personal sector and small- to medium-sized businesses – normally confined to the bank's local region. Deposits are guaranteed by the

Savings Bank Association. Their central organizations, Girozentralle, even out liquidity between different savings banks and act as large universal banks. The credit co-operatives, originally established to help agriculture and crafts, now pursue a full range of banking activities through their central organization, collectively accounting for 17.0 per cent of banking assets. Mortgage banks account for 14.2 per cent of total assets. Foreign banks account for a relatively small share of banking assets. De-regulation of banking started much earlier in Germany, capital movements being largely free since the late 1950s, interest rate regulations abolished in 1967, and the coupon tax on non-residents' income from holding bonds in 1984. During 1985 and 1986 the Deutsche Bundesbank further relaxed international capital market requirements and made rule changes which have attracted foreign investment banks.

In contrast the UK has far fewer banks, many having specific market orientation. At the end of February 1987 there were 588 authorized banking institutions, of which 298 were recognized banks (the balance being licensed institutions), with a mean asset size of £1,032mn and a median asset size of £121mn. The international importance of Britain as a banking centre is seen in 254 being overseas institutions with UK branches, 67 UK incorporated subsidiaries of overseas banks and 23 UK incorporated joint ventures between overseas institutions and in some cases between overseas and UK institutions. The main domestic and personal banking business is handled through the retail commercial banks (the London and Scottish clearing banks and the TSB Group) with corporate finance work through the accepting houses/merchant banks. Until 1981 mortgage business was mostly done through the building societies but banks in the 1980s attained a significant share of the house finance market. Overseas banks and branches of foreign financial institutions specialize in Euro-currency and trade finance. As at end-March 1987 retail banks accounted for 24.8 per cent of banking assets, accepting houses 3.7 per cent, Japanese banks 26.3 per cent and US banks 10.8 per cent. A major feature of the 1980s has been the declining significance of the US banks and the rise of Japanese-owned banks to the extent that they are collectively in terms of overall assets and liabilities more important than the domestic retail banks. During the 1980s the distinctions between the types of banks have become more blurred with many shareholding inter-relationships between banks in different categories, the development of merchant banking subsidiaries of the retail/clearing banks and the ability to buy Stock Exchange member firms from 1986. Banking is controlled by the Bank of England with the Banking Acts of 1979 and 1986 giving statutory backing especially with regard to capital requirements. De-regulation has gathered pace since the adoption of credit and competition control in 1971 which ended the clearing banks' interest rate cartel, the ending of exchange control in 1979, the Stock Exchange and capital markets reforms of 1986 and the provisions of the 1986 Financial Services Act. The 1979 Banking Act was due to be replaced in 1987, major provisions of the new Act including revised capital requirements and the re-categorization of banks into a single category.

Banking in France is highly concentrated with the top four banks accounting for 80 per cent of deposits and little competition between financial intermediaries; many banks are nationalized, with some mutual banks enjoying preferential tax treatment and 'captive' markets. There are three main types of banks – commercial, specialist and savings and until 1984 commercial banks were catergorized into deposit banks; banques d'affaires (investment banks); and banques de crédit à long et moyen terme. Under Law No. 84–46 the categories disappeared and banks were redefined as établissements de crédit, competition being encouraged between each institution and with the intention to move eventually towards a system of universal banking. Ownership of banks differs from most of Western Europe with large- and medium-sized banks being nationalized (the latest round of nationalization being only in 1982) while many of the others are semi-public or co-operative institutions. The period of nationalization has resulted in the capital bases of the banks being lower than is common in many other banking centres although in 1987 a programme of privatization of some of the nationalized banks commenced, led by the very successful flotation of Paribas. Until recently there had been little competition between the financial intermediaries with high lending rates and low deposit rates, although reforms in 1971 had sought to reduce the scale of fixed-rate refinancing and increase the role of the money market rate. Acts of 1978 and 1983 encouraged the use of the Stock Market for raising finance while the 1984 Banking Act was aimed at increasing banking competition. Since then, bank credits have been gradually de-subsidized, new reserve requirements introduced, the system of quantitative credit limits ended, the banks allowed to offer tax-exempt savings products like other institutions, free negotiation of bonds and brokerage fees introduced, banks empowered to issue Certificates of Deposit and companies to issue commercial paper, the opening of a financial futures exchange, reform of the inter-bank market, and domestic financial markets gradually opened up to foreigners by relaxation of exchange control procedures. The proportion of the population with a bank account is among the highest of West European countries, with the usage of cheques the highest. From January 1987 banks have been allowed to charge for services – 'tarification'. Banks are not allowed to have more than 10 per cent of their operations in non-banking activities.

Italian banking is generally de-centralized with over 1,000 commercial banks operating. The largest banks operate on a national scale dealing with medium and large companies and more recently developing retail branch networks. Commercial banks fall into seven main categories: public law banks owned by either the state or foundations with a network of special credit institution subsidiaries; banks of national interest controlled by the Istituto per la Riconstruzione Industriale; ordinary credit banks, rather smaller institutions normally on a joint-stock basis; foreign banks which are highly regulated by the Bank of Italy; savings banks and first-class pledge banks; and two types of co-operative banks – people's banks and rural and artisan banks. Much of the structure of the banking system still depends on the 1936 Banking Act but major reforms were confirmed in May 1987 to encourage merchant banking, allowing banks to purchase equity stakes in companies, to facilitate banks bringing companies to the Stock Exchange and underwriting bonds and stocks; allowing certain categories of commercial banks to offer medium- and long-term loans in competition with the industrial investment banks; a loosening of the rules restricting commercial banks from creating branches outside their immediate region; and allowing foreign banks to compete for loan business more widely. Although the financial services sector is still relatively underdeveloped, banks since 1984 have found more competition from leasing, factoring and other financial service companies, while unit trusts have been in operation since 1984. Exchange controls, which have been extremely strict, are being relaxed.

As in Germany the Swiss banking system is universal but with five basic groups of banks; the big banks, the five largest, which are also very strong in international banking; the cantonal banks aimed at the requirements of business, government and commerce and mortgage finance within the individual cantons; the regional and savings banks; mutual and local banks (Raiffeisen) represented by two umbrella organizations; and other banking intermediaries, some of which are foreign owned, specializing in portfolio management, placement of securities and wholesale banking. The five big banks account for about half of the total banking assets, two-thirds of foreign assets and one-third of mortgage advances. Other banks are roughly equal with cantonal banks at 19 per cent of total assets but with others accounting for just over 30 per cent of foreign assets and cantonal banks for 38 per cent of mortgages. Banking is controlled by the Federal Banking Commission under the Swiss Bank Acts with the regulation of credit being the responsibility of the Swiss National Bank, with regulatory aspects of banking tending to be liberal. In 1986 the financial services market was helped by the lifting of the sales tax on physical gold transactions, the repeal of the 35 per cent withholding tax on inter-bank transactions, the halving of the stamp duty on Eurobond issues and several other measures relaxing external capital market and securities issues.

In the Netherlands the mid-1980s have seen an expansion of merchant banking activities and the de-regulation of the capital markets and the insurance industry. In Austria, following some liberalization in the 1970s, a new banking law in 1987 sought to increase capital ratios, partially by the creation of new types of participation and subordinated capital. In Denmark financial markets were broadly liberalized by 1985 when restrictions on inward and outward indirect investment were lifted and domestic market quantitative regulations were ended, being replaced by market-related controls. In Sweden price and volume controls on bank lending were abolished in 1985 and foreign banks were allowed to establish operations in addition to representative offices in 1986, the number of commercial banks operating doubling in the year to 24. Exchange controls remain more stringent than in any other European countries. Norway has also seen considerable de-regulation since 1985, while in Finland there is now almost total interest rate competition, new financial instruments have been introduced and many foreign exchange regulations ended. Belgian banking is one of the most technically advanced in Europe but has a very high number of branches for the size of the population.

Throughout Europe there has been considerable expansion of

banking activities during the 1980s. Growth of deposits has been considerable in many countries (Table 5.2) with demand deposits more than doubling between the ends of 1980 and 1986 in Iceland, Luxembourg, UK, Norway, Greece, Denmark and Finland. Time and savings deposits also grew considerably, doubling in all these same countries (other than Norway) as well as Portugal. The relative hard currency countries such as Germany, Switzerland and the Netherlands had lower rates of growth reflecting the comparative successes of monetary and counter-inflation policies.

TABLE 5.2   GROWTH OF BANK DEPOSITS IN EUROPEAN COUNTRIES

	Demand deposits			Time and savings deposits		
	1980	1986	Growth (%)	1980	1986	Growth (%)
Austria (Sch bn)	73.5	105.7	43.8	620.0	1012.4	63.3
Belgium (B Fcs bn)	293.7	444.7	51.4	771.4	1263.9	63.8
Denmark (Kr bn)	53.3	137.0	157.0	53.08	107.89	103.3
Finland (Mk mn)	10673	21945	105.6	65600	141073	115.1
France (F Fcs bn)	429	723	68.5	675	1067	58.1
Germany (DM bn)	158.8	227.2	43.1	560.5	804.1	42.9
Greece (Dr bn)	75.9	199.2	162.5	544.7	2298.7	321.6
Iceland (Kr mn)	768	20822	2549.1	2993	29297	878.8
Ireland (I£ mn)	817.3	1076.9	31.8	2992.5	5459.2	82.4
Italy (L '000 bn)	141.40	142.22	71.3	113.9	195.4	40.3
Luxembourg (Fcs mn)	22.4	85.3	280.8	181.6	394.9	117.2
Netherlands (G mn)	43.54	67.56	55.2	170.65	241.16	41.3
Norway (Kr bn)	22.53	64.46	186.1	104.59	180.77	72.8
Portugal (Esc bn)	337.98	581.48	72.0	624.92	1888.27	202.2
Spain (Ps bn)	2882	4881	69.4	8221	14448	75.7
Switzerland (Sw Fcs bn)	27.19	34.46	27.3	115.12	211.31	83.6
UK* (£bn)	20.81	61.66	196.3	43.74	108.93	149.0

* Includes foreign currency deposits
Note: 1986 data refer to end-November for the Netherlands; to end-September for Belgium, Denmark, Finland, France and Norway; to end-June for Italy and Switzerland; and to end-June 1985 for Portugal
Source: International financial statistics

Broadly similar trends can also be seen in bank lending, with bank claims on the private sector (Table 5.3) more than doubling in the same period in Denmark, Finland, Greece, Iceland, Luxembourg, Norway, Portugal and the UK. German, Austrian and Belgian lending grew at a slower rate than deposit taking.

TABLE 5.3 GROWTH OF BANK CLAIMS ON THE PRIVATE SECTOR

	1980	1986	Growth (%)
Austria (Sch bn)	754.2	874.6	16.0
Belgium (B Fcs bn)	1011.2	1235.1	22.1
Denmark (Kr bn)	157.44	346.42	120.0
Finland (Mk mn)	92733	230363	148.4
France (F Fcs bn)	1361	2267	66.6
Germany (DM bn)	1156.7	1597.0	38.1
Greece (Dr bn)	771.7	1816.4	135.4
Iceland (Kr mn)	4309	55112	1179.0
Ireland (I£ mn)	2948.0	4343.8	47.3
Italy (L '000 bn)	136.72	259.15	89.5
Luxembourg (Fcs mn)	1144.9	2450.7	114.1
Netherlands (G mn)	225.18	288.89	27.4
Norway (Kr bn)	97.23	278.18	187.4
Portugal (Esc bn)	698.89	1637.22	134.3
Spain (Ps bn)	10719	17074	59.3
Switzerland (Sw Fcs bn)	195.78	342.61	75.0
UK (£bn)	56.58	141.06	149.3

Note: For Luxembourg and the Netherlands, 1986 data refer to end-November; for Denmark, Finland, Greece, Iceland, Norway and Sweden 1986 to end-September; for Italy and Switzerland end-June; and for Portugal June 1985.
Source: International financial statistics

While regulation of banks remains essentially a matter for national central monetary institutions (and finance ministries), there are two formal committees within the EC to cover this aspect among member countries: the Banking Advisory Committee established under the 1977 First Banking Co-ordination Directive, and the Contact Group of EC Supervisory Authorities. These two groups have developed observation ratios relating to solvency, profitability and liquidity of banking institutions in member states, while the Contact Group was examining in 1987 activities of banking institutions in the broader financial spheres of insurance, securities and investment businesses. Within the EC a free market in banking services is due to be achieved by 1992. In December 1986 the Council of Ministers adopted a Directive for the standardization of banks' accounts and Recommendations (which do not have the force of law) on large exposures and deposit guarantee schemes, while in mid-1987 draft Directives were being discussed on capital, the winding up and reorganization of credit institutions, and on mortgage credit.

III Investment flows and international aspects of European banking

With the development of the Euro-currency markets since the late 1950s, the method of balance of payments financing for many European countries has radically changed with a decreasing reliance on support through stand-by and other credit facilities from the International Monetary Fund. Deficits can now frequently be financed through use of the Euro-markets either through bank borrowing or the issue of Eurobonds.

The early 1980s produced a series of serious current account deficits for most of the European countries other than Switzerland and the three gas and oil producers, the Netherlands, Norway and the UK (Table 5.4). For many of the deficit countries this shortfall was covered by positive inflows of both short- and long-term capital raised on the Euro-markets either through short-term bank facilities, medium- and long-term syndicated bank loans and the issue of Eurobonds. By 1985 the pattern of current account balances had changed substantially with most European countries back in surplus, West Germany dramatically so. Short- and long-term capital accounts also showed major changes as a result and also taking account of the final period of US dollar appreciation. Notably there were very serious overall net long- and short-term outflows from West Germany, the Netherlands, Switzerland and the UK.

Crucial to the financing of these deficits in recent years has been the use made of the Euro-currency markets. These grew up from very small origins in the late 1950s representing external currency deposits in a different currency from the banking country in which they were deposited and re-lent. In the 1960s and 1970s Euro-currency transactions were mostly dollar denominated, much of the market being on an inter-bank basis with non-bank lending taking the form of medium- and long-term syndicated loans to foreign governments, or government guaranteed institutions and companies. Eurobonds, an equivalent bond market, developed in the 1960s with a secondary market created for subsequent trading. With the advent of the international debt crisis affecting many developing countries, there was a sharp decrease in syndicated lending to such countries, a shift to lending a higher proportion of funds to well respected European borrowers and the securitization of debt, partially through higher usage of the Eurobond market than normal

TABLE 5.4   CURRENT AND CAPITAL ACCOUNTS OF
             EUROPEAN COUNTRIES

in SDRmn

Borrowers	Current account 1981	Current account 1985	Long-term capital 1981	Long-term capital 1985	Short-term capital 1981	Short-term capital 1985
Austria	−1239	−226	799	−149	522	−424
Belgium–Luxembourg	−3544	614	3148	−4770	−922	4558
Denmark	−1582	−2667	1147	4389	53	276
Finland	−335	−648	473	1267	−487	−42
France	−4057	738	−7650	3690	9468	−2101
West Germany	−4230	13294	2786	−2187	1346	−14024
Greece	−2023	−2071	1357	2825	190	404
Iceland	−2189	−	165	152	34	77
Ireland	−	−	1960	−	69	−
Italy	−7108	−4143	6902	2489	76	715
Netherlands	3080	5306	−2516	−3613	−667	−64
Norway	1840	2918	−624	−687	−832	2402
Portugal	−2183	−490	1052	984	−54	−167
Spain	−4140	2921	3566	−1339	1490	−1870
Sweden	−2437	−1061	−920	−5000	1418	2282
Switzerland	1235	6112	−8160	−6570	1905	−1666
United Kingdom	10894	5076	−14978	−16928	3948	8893

Source: – Balance of Payments Yearbook

international banking syndicated loans. The majority of European countries have had favoured credit ratings and consequently the Euromarkets have represented a favourable way for financing balance of payment deficits either on a syndicated lending basis or through the issue of Eurobonds.

A measure of the success of the international banking community in raising funds can be seen in Table 5.5 (p82) which shows the total funds raised on the international markets by European countries in the years 1981 to 1986. While there have been sharp fluctuations on a year-to-year basis, the most significant borrowers have been Denmark, France, Italy, Sweden and the UK, although West Germany was a large borrower in 1986. EEC institutions, notably the EIB, have also made extensive use of the international financial markets. The two most important components of this international finance raising, bond issues and medium- and long-term banking facilities, are shown in Tables 5.6 and 5.7.

This has of course led to substantial external liabilities and claims of banks vis à vis European countries. Net lending has been done by

TABLE 5.5   FUNDS RAISED ON THE INTERNATIONAL MARKETS

in $mn

Borrowers	1981	1982	1983	1984	1985	1986
Austria	1967	1974	1741	2232	2434	3580
Belgium	994	2381	1325	2702	3269	4952
Denmark	2418	2643	4679	5596	3589	9632
Finland	1243	871	1161	1658	1845	3445
France	6941	15149	11363	12103	18772	19700
West Germany	344	1401	2998	2063	3452	11927
Greece	1028	981	1383	1324	1587	1317
Iceland	105	321	118	284	304	427
Ireland	1541	1623	1782	1794	1881	4179
Italy	8728	6874	4720	8855	11033	12962
Luxembourg	60	347	208	129	103	225
Netherlands	1037	1134	1255	1399	2298	3579
Norway	1428	2276	1550	2685	3905	6644
Portugal	1706	1952	1136	1752	2381	2432
Spain	5293	3021	4452	5380	3912	7015
Sweden	4230	4552	4867	13109	9889	8020
Switzerland	–	610	855	1683	864	1947
United Kingdom	3945	3491	3416	9524	25424	24295
Council of Europe	196	457	396	464	348	733
ECSC	252	325	387	278	408	1018
EEC	303	573	4756	685	2882	1271
EIB	1649	2162	2423	2602	3666	5223
Euratom	289	330	176	105	45	505
Global Total	200553	178928	157827	228774	284719	317557

Source: OECD

TABLE 5.6   INTERNATIONAL MEDIUM- AND LONG-TERM BANK LOANS

in $mn

Borrowers	1981	1982	1983	1984	1985	1986
Austria	460	527	213	100	663	–
Belgium	466	1981	50	800	536	500
Denmark	1578	753	1886	370	108	132
Finland	492	26	285	–	104	40
France	630	5958	473	1484	3873	3229
West Germany	100	–	36	–	39	115
Greece	959	931	1088	1065	470	1015
Iceland	70	163	–	263	7	381
Ireland	1025	702	684	757	259	1370
Italy	6252	4425	2588	4509	4524	5615
Luxembourg	–	35	–	20	–	–
Netherlands	253	255	70	234	16	280
Norway	832	1441	811	1410	1442	176
Portugal	1656	1355	964	806	1486	1357
Spain	4445	1844	2284	2305	2420	4333
Sweden	1671	1947	2481	331	315	45
United Kingdom	2559	2162	913	3363	5073	2243
EEC	–	–	1240	–	–	–
Euratom	–	–	–	–	30	–
Global Total	91263	90751	60208	53218	53461	49946

Source: OECD

TABLE 5.7 INTERNATIONAL ISSUES OF BONDS

in $mn Issuers	1981	1982	1983	1984	1985	1986
Austria	598	993	852	1691	1965	2415
Belgium	250	100	910	1626	2225	3866
Denmark	363	744	1772	3548	2865	8512
Finland	222	389	343	1105	1226	3022
France	2277	6918	6103	7020	10240	12509
West Germany	110	1364	2451	1660	3065	10184
Greece	30	50	–	150	644	68
Iceland	–	83	–	–	220	46
Ireland	419	560	826	736	1349	1741
Italy	1110	837	1204	3587	4993	4841
Luxembourg	15	270	–	119	103	225
Netherlands	294	759	1112	1034	1159	2725
Norway	182	396	454	966	2185	5246
Portugal	20	140	55	200	185	120
Spain	298	334	986	1180	1183	1491
Sweden	947	1619	3366	3983	4494	4872
Switzerland	–	600	845	496	864	1947
United Kingdom	1229	1089	1525	4736	14987	18538
Council of Europe	–	56	32	71	231	473
ECSC	40	80	75	207	195	826
EEC	140	200	2947	299	2234	1087
EIB	461	572	953	1091	1606	2786
Euratom	188	55	46	–	33	419
Global Total	31279	50370	50098	81717	135430	186952

Source: OECD

banks in Switzerland, the UK, Germany and the Netherlands (Table 5.8 p84) with Italy and France being the largest European debtor countries towards the banks, with liabilities of $33.9bn and $30.1bn at the end of 1986. Clearly the UK and Swiss positions with net assets of $83.4bn and $193.3bn are special, reflecting in addition to their balance of payments positions considerations such as major international financial centres. The German position is all the more remarkable in that, having been a net debtor to the international banking system as recently as the end of 1983, it became in 1985–86 the largest supplier of funds to the international banking market, providing $48bn in 1986 alone.

Although the Euro-markets originated in Paris and Milan in the mid-1950s it was the UK which during the 1960s became the most important centre, providing the correct mix of skills, infrastructure and the correct language for the many US banks involved. Potential

**TABLE 5.8   EXTERNAL POSITIONS OF BANKS IN EUROPEAN BIS
REPORTING COUNTRIES, END 1986**

in $mn Liabilities/assets vis à vis	Liabilities	Assets	Net
Austria	24557	33581	9024
Belgium/Luxembourg	154155	166935	12780
Denmark	13579	33886	10207
Finland	5390	14742	9352
France	106318	136547	30129
West Germany	139804	104023	(35881)
Greece	6805	14314	7509
Republic of Ireland	5965	13653	7688
Italy	60277	94218	33941
Netherlands	73789	52237	(21552)
Norway	6968	23707	16739
Portugal	5330	10459	5129
Switzerland (incl. BIS)	254269	60928	(193341)
United Kingdom	450259	366881	(83378)
Yugoslavia	2318	10298	7970

Source: Bank for International Settlements and Bank of England

rival centres such as Zurich and Frankfurt suffered from their domestic sales taxation system, helping to make London a more attractive base. Consequently the UK emerged as the leading international banking centre in Europe (Table 5.9), a position it has maintained in the 1980s despite moves to liberalization of controls elsewhere and the aims of, for instance, France to develop its international financial community. In 1986 the UK's share of the global international banking market was still almost four times that of its nearest rival, France.

In addition to the Eurobond market, increasing emphasis was being paid in the mid-1980s to the international marketability of equities, the Euro-equity market. With the relaxation of exchange control regulations, institutional investors were prepared to invest more readily in foreign equities. A growing number of prime European companies started to issue equity on a syndicated international basis among investment banks, while the broadening of financial groups in London following the Stock Exchange reforms in 1986 has resulted in a substantial expansion of the foreign equity business, with turnover estimated in mid-1987 at a level of at least

TABLE 5.9   MAJOR EUROPEAN COUNTRIES INTERNATIONAL BANKING

	Gross lending	Percentage share of global international banking		
	Total $bn	End-Dec 1984	1985	1986
Belgium	160	3.3	3.8	3.9
Luxembourg	168	3.7	4.0	4.1
France	241	6.7	6.6	5.9
West Germany	161	2.4	3.1	3.9
Italy	83	2.1	2.1	2.0
Netherlands	101	2.4	2.5	2.5
Switzerland	108	2.2	2.5	2.6
Swiss trustee accounts	137*	3.7	3.7	3.3
United Kingdom	957	24.3	24.5	23.3

Source: Bank for International Settlements and Bank of England

£1bn a day mostly centred around 100 stocks and accounting for 40-50 per cent of London equity turnover and, according to some estimates, one-third of the turnover of the ten main stocks in most European markets. This also highlights the dominant role of the UK in the European Stock Market league (Table 5.10 p86) with the largest number of companies traded and highest market capitalization and turnover, although in a global context the UK lies significantly behind Tokyo and New York on turnover and market value; after the UK, the next most important markets are Paris, Germany and Zurich, although Basle has the largest number of overseas companies quoted on its exchange. In general London benefits from being able to trade large blocks of shares (often in units of over $1mn) which local European markets, often relatively illiquid, over regulated and over taxed, are not able to do. Reforms are under way to modernize the technology and structure in many European countries, ensuring that national markets are ready to stand up to competition as the EC's target for internal market competition is achieved in 1992. France, for instance, has launched a five-year plan under which from 1990 outside investors will be allowed to own 100 per cent of the equity of the 45 Parisian and 15 regional firms of stockbrokers.

While international banking and financial markets are to some extent controlled by overall capital requirements in the individual banking centre or as an extension of the regulatory environment of

TABLE 5.10   EUROPEAN STOCK MARKETS, 1986

	Market Value £mn	Turnover £mn	Companies number
Amsterdam[a]	121028	39024	509
Athens[a]	2930	26	114
Barcelona	59036	1876	411
Basle[b]	114885	n/a	899
Brussels	77451	7120	331
Copenhagen	93078	10441	281
Geneva[b]	115144	48594	329
Germany (Association of Exchanges)	n/a	211234	673
Helsinki	13261	1134	52
Luxembourg	18557	432	421
Madrid	58193	10842	312
Milan	282479	37497	184
Oslo	22527	12346	155
Paris	314607	241446	1100
Stockholm	n/a	17233	156
UK[a]	481882	323133	2613
Vienna	33761	4071	113
Zurich[b]	131173	117153	339

[a] Turnover has been halved for comparison purposes
[b] Turnover includes off-floor transactions of various kinds and is partly accounted for on both the buyer and seller sides
n/a Not Available
Note: Market value is at year end and comprises total domestic fixed interest and equity; turnover is for the year 1986 and includes fixed interest and equity; number of companies includes both domestic and overseas companies quoted on the stock market
Source: The Stock Exchange

the country of origin of the bank, proper international supervision is still a matter of concern. Outside the formal EC structure outlined in the previous section, the Bank of International Settlements (the BIS) in Basle holds monthly meetings for central bank governors of the Group of Ten countries. It also organizes periodic meetings of central bank officials to examine important aspects of banking practice and supervision. The BIS Committee on Banking Regulations and Supervisory Practices regularly reviews supervisory developments in individual countries, examining during 1985–87 in particular measures of international banks' capital adequacy and the growth of their off-balance sheet business.

IV   Currencies and the European Monetary System

With European countries highly interdependent economically, financially and in trade it has long been seen as a priority to limit the fluctuations in currency exchange rates between the various member states of the EC and with other countries through the normal international forums such as the International Monetary Fund and the Bank for International Settlements. Within the EC a concerted attempt has been made since 1972 to limit currency fluctuations between member states through the Snake and the European Monetary System. The Snake was established in April 1972 to keep the fluctuations of European currencies within narrower limits than allowed by the end-1971 (IMF) Smithsonian Agreements by the six then members of the EEC with the UK, Ireland, Denmark and Norway also joining. The early days of the Snake were relatively disastrous with the UK and Italy being forced to withdraw in the first few months and France in 1974 because of exchange rate pressures. Additionally, there were at the time serious underlying national political, economic and monetary worries by the member countries. In December 1978 the European Council formally took the decision to establish a European Monetary System (EMS), to create closer monetary co-operation leading to a zone of monetary stability in Europe. The decisive political impetus for a new attempt to stabilize intra-EC exchange rates had come from a Franco-German initiative earlier in the year and was influenced by the growing weakness of the US dollar and the destabilizing influence this exerted on exchange rates between European currencies.

The EMS became operative in March 1979 envisaging a durable and effective exchange rate system comprising all European currencies in which the European Currency Unit, ecu, would play a central role as a standard of reference for central exchange rates and a common denominator of claims and liabilities arising from official interventions in EEC currencies. Ecu assets were to be created against the receipt of dollars and gold from participants, monetary reserves and, at a later date, against national currencies, and were to be used as a means of settlement among EC central banks. The exchange rate mechanism defines for the participating currencies their central exchange rates, intervention limits and intervention procedures. Participants declare a central rate for their currency in terms of the ecu, a standard basket of fixed amounts of the EC currencies (see Table 5.11) reflecting countries' individual shares of intra-European trade, gross national products and quotas in the EEC's short-term monetary support arrangements. Each pair of EEC currencies' bilateral central exchange rate is derived from the currencies' ecu central rates with the margin of fluctuation on either side of the bilateral central rates limited to 2¼ per cent (for mid-1987 rates see Table 5.12) for all the currencies which were members of the Snake; for other EEC currencies margins of up to 6 per cent could be applied. To back up the intervention limits major short- and medium-term credit facilities were agreed by the EEC. The most important country to decide not to participate in the EMS was the United Kingdom.

TABLE 5.11   COMPOSITION OF THE ECU BASKET

		13/3/79	17/9/84
Deutschmark	1 ECU =	0.828	0.719
French Franc		1.15	1.31
Dutch Florin		0.286	0.256
Belgian Franc		3.66	3.71
Luxembourg Franc		0.14	0.14
Italian Lira		109	140
Danish Kroner		0.217	0.219
Irish Punt		0.00759	0.00871
Pound Sterling		0.0885	0.0878
Greek Drachma		–	1.15

Source: Eurostat

Between the start of the EMS and mid-1987 there had been 13 re-alignments of the currencies, only one of which was caused by the inclusion of a new member, Greece in 1984, which also prompted a revision of the currency basket composition of the ecu (Table 5.11). These re-alignments have reflected general international exchange rate developments, frequently, but not always, the appreciation of the Deutschmark against other EC currencies. The inclusion of currencies with very different domestic economic backgrounds will inevitably cause strains despite the long-term movement towards greater co-ordination of economic, counter-inflation and monetary policy among EC member countries. Since 1979 there has been a gradual narrowing of differences of economic policies in the EC with lower and closer rates of both monetary growth and inflation,

TABLE 5.12   EMS: BILATERAL CENTRAL RATES AND INTERVENTION POINTS*
(in use since 12/01/87)

		Amster-dam in HFL	Brussels in B/LFR	Frankfurt in DM	Copen-hagen in DKR	Dublin in IRL	Paris en FF	Rome in LIT
100 HFL	+2·25%	100	1872·15	90·7700	346·240	33·8868	304·440	67912·0
	cent. rate		1830·54	88·7526	338·537	33·1293	297·661	63963·1
	-2·25%		1789·85	86·7800	331·020	32·3939	291·040	60241·0
100 B/LFR	+2·25%	5·58700	100	4·95900	18·9143	1·85100	16·6310	3710·20
	cent. rate	5·46286		4·84837	18·4938	1·80981	16·2608	3494·21
	-2·25%	5·34150		4·74000	18·0831	1·76950	15·8990	3290·90
100 DM	+2·25%	115·235	2109·50	100	390·160	38·1825	343·050	76540·0
	cent. rate	112·673	2062·55		381·443	37·3281	335·386	72069·9
	-2·25%	110·1675	2016·55		373·000	36·4964	327·920	67865·0
100 DKR	+2·25%	30·2100	553·000	26·8100	100	10·0087	89·9250	20062·0
	cent. rate	29·5389	540·723	26·2162		9·7860	87·9257	18894·0
	-2·25%	28·8825	528·700	25·6300		9·5683	85·9700	17794·0
1 IRL	+2·25%	3·08700	56·5115	2·74000	10·4511	1	9·1890	2050·03
	cent. rate	3·01848	55·2545	2·67894	10·2186		8·8948	1930·71
	-2·25%	2·95100	54·0250	2·61900	9·9913		8·7850	1818·34
100 FF	+2·25%	34·3600	628·970	30·4950	116·320	11·3830	100	22817·0
	cent. rate	33·5953	614·977	29·8164	113·732	11·1299		21488·6
	-2·25%	32·8475	601·295	29·1500	111·200	10·8825		20238·0
1000 LIT	+6%	1·6600	30·3870	1·47350	5·62000	0·549952	4·94100	1000
	cent. rate	1·5634	28·6187	1·38754	5·29268	0·517943	4·65362	
	-6%	1·4725	26·9530	1·30650	4·98500	0·487799	4·38300	
1 ECU	cent. rate	2·31943	42·4582	2·05853	7·85212	0·768411	6·90403	1483·58

* The UKL and the DR do not participate in the exchange rate mechanism of the EMS. Their theoretical central rates are respectively: 0·739615 UKL and 150·792 DR.
Source: Eurostat

which has helped to lower previous high rates of currency fluctuation. Nevertheless, in each year since the creation of the EMS, West Germany has had an inflation rate significantly lower than the other EMS members, the lowest differential, in 1986, still being 3.5 per cent. Against this background it is an achievement that the EMS had not been subject to more internal pressures.

Many of the pressures which have afflicted EMS currencies in the 1980s are also evident in the performance of other European currencies. Currency management of non-members of the EMS tends to take account of EMS movements while intervention to support major non-member currencies, notably the pound sterling, may take place through agreements made between central bankers on either a formal or informal basis, e.g. through the regular meetings of Central Bank Governors held at the Bank for International Settlements, or meetings of the Finance Ministers and Central Bank Governors of the Group of Five and Group of Ten countries. Between 1980, when the policy of the United States Federal Reserve Bank changed initiating a period of dollar strength fuelled by a large increase in US interest rates and a highly expansionary fiscal policy, and the dollar's peak in early 1985 European currencies came under considerable pressure, aggravated by the effects of the oil crisis on levels of economic activity, inflation and balance of payments. Effects of these factors varied from country to country depending on its ability to produce oil and counter-cyclical and counter-inflationary policies. Nevertheless, the overall weakness of the European currencies during this period can be seen in no single European currency having an average effective exchange rate in 1985 better than in 1980 (Table 5.13). However, in 1986 as the extent of the US dollar's new-found weakness became apparent, the Austrian schilling, Deutchmark, guilder and Swiss franc moved decisively to higher effective rates than in 1980, the Swiss franc having been the consistently most strong European currency in the early 1980s, helped by its traditional conservative economic and monetary policies and low inflation, and reaching the highest effective exchange rate in 1986. In contrast, the weakest currencies have been Spain and Italy, both having lost over 30 per cent of their 1980 value, while Sweden, France and the UK have lost around a quarter. The two major European oil producers saw weakening of their currencies in 1986 against the strengthening trend in other European currencies.

TABLE 5.13   AVERAGE EFFECTIVE EXCHANGE RATES OF
             MAJOR EUROPEAN CURRENCIES

Country	1981	1982	1983	1984	1985	1986
Austria	91.8	94.0	94.7	91.2	91.3	102.6
Belgium	93.2	84.1	80.7	78.2	78.7	83.6
Denmark	90.0	85.1	83.4	79.2	80.4	88.8
Finland	96.0	94.7	86.4	85.0	85.0	87.0
France	89.4	81.3	74.2	69.7	70.4	74.7
Germany	92.7	96.5	98.8	96.1	95.9	106.4
Ireland	89.2	86.5	81.4	76.5	77.5	83.2
Italy	86.7	80.2	76.1	71.1	67.0	69.5
Netherlands	93.2	97.0	97.8	94.8	95.2	105.7
Norway	96.7	94.9	89.1	85.3	83.4	81.3
Spain	88.4	81.9	66.7	64.0	62.3	63.7
Sweden	94.7	84.1	72.9	72.6	72.2	73.1
Switzerland	96.6	102.7	104.8	100.3	99.2	111.5
UK	98.9	94.2	86.7	81.9	81.5	75.9

Note: 1980 = 100
Source: International financial statistics

A further aspect of currencies is their comparative use in international trade and banking. During the 1980s the use of most European currencies and the Japanese yen increased significantly at the expense of the US dollar, whose share in the cross-border positions of banks declined from nearly 75 per cent at the end of 1984 to 58.5 per cent at end-1986. The share of the Deutschmark in external lending by BIS area banks rose to 12.8 per cent of amounts outstanding at the end of 1986, the Swiss franc to 6.3 per cent, the pound sterling to 3.6 per cent and the ecu to 2.1 per cent. In terms of shares of international issues of bonds (Table 5.14 p92) the Deutschmark accounted for 9 per cent of 1986 issues, the pound sterling 5.6 per cent and the ecu 3.7 per cent. Of particular interest has been the use of ecu denominated transactions (totalling some $54.2bn at end-1985) with the market becoming broad in terms of geographical spread and non-bank participation in 1985–86. The BIS in March 1986 agreed to establish itself as an agent of a new private ecu clearing and settlement system set up by the Ecu Banking Association.

TABLE 5.14   INTERNATIONAL ISSUES OF BONDS BY CURRENCY OF ISSUE

in US $ mn Currency	1981	1982	1983	1984	1985	1986
Belgian Franc	–	137	–	–	–	6
Danish Kroner	–	–	–	–	458	1121
Deutschmark	1396	3252	4042	4324	9491	16869
Dutch Guilder	446	618	747	986	681	916
ECUs	153	823	2191	2938	7038	6965
French Franc	513	–	–	–	1058	3398
Italian Lira	–	–	–	–	84	329
Norwegian Kroner	53	31	67	156	147	26
Pound Sterling	535	846	2153	3964	5766	10510
Global Total	31279	50370	50098	81717	135430	186952

Source: OECD

V   Exchange controls

For much of the post-war era, many European economies have been
subjected to strict exchange control regulations reflecting not just
the discouragement of capital and current outflows for the weak
currencies but also the discouragement of inflows for the stronger
currencies. Although the European Community envisaged freedom
of movement of capital between member countries and free
competition in financial markets, it has been only in the mid-1980s
that de-regulation of controls has really started, with the UK's
abolition of exchange controls (but not certain aspects of its capital
markets) in 1979 being a turning point. Since then there has been
considerable liberalization of regulations although countries such as
France and Italy still maintain a complex system of exchange control
restrictions. Italian controls were being relaxed in mid-1987 but
residents were still not allowed to have foreign bank accounts, there
were limits on personal travel allowances and exporters and
importers were not wholly free to cover forward in forward
exchange markets. Similarly, in France major exchange controls
had been eased in 1986 although some restrictions such as personal
tourist allowances still remained in force albeit at a less punitive
level. Important regulatory changes affecting international capital
market activity took place in Germany, Italy and France in 1985–86
expanding the international Deutschmark bond issue market, re-

opening the Euro-French franc bond market and allowing Italian lire bond issues by non-residents.

Within the EC progress to harmonization and the ending of restrictions was seen in the agreement reached in February 1986 to complete the common internal market by the end of 1992. The Council of Ministers in November 1986 adopted a Directive to liberalize those capital transactions that directly relate to the functioning of the Common Market and the regulation of the national capital markets within the second stage complete freedom of capital transactions within the Community being established. Initially these measures relate directly to the functioning of the EC and the regulation of internal capital markets with secondly the complete freedom of capital transactions within the EC, relating in particular to the admission of financial credits, money market transactions and deposits on bank accounts as well as the abolition of two-tier foreign exchange rate markets and any discrimination in cross-border capital transactions.

CHAPTER SIX
INDUSTRIAL DEVELOPMENT IN EUROPE

Those who stress the importance of industry as the major source of dynamism in the economy often choose to describe that sector as the 'engine room of growth'. Industrial growth, in turn, is closely related to the pattern and nature of structural change within the sector. Other prominent determinants of industrial performance are the availability of natural resources, including energy, and the role of industrial investment and capital expenditures. Each of these subjects is examined in the following sections. The chapter concludes with a discussion of the industrial outlook in West Europe.

I   Manufacturing output

Growth of manufacturing output in Western Europe accelerated in 1986, rising at a faster pace than GDP in most countries. Indices of industrial production are given in Table 6.1. They reaffirm the general observation made in Chapter 1 that much of the growth since 1983 merely offset the contraction in output which occurred during the previous downswing. As recently as 1984, production in France, Greece, Italy, Switzerland and West Germany had still not reached levels of 1980. When the years 1980–86 are regarded as a single period, only a few of the smaller economies – Finland, Ireland, Norway, Portugal and Sweden – managed rates of growth in excess of 2 per cent.

Long-term changes in the composition of manufacturing output are closely related to the pace of growth. The direction of causation, however, is a two-way affair. In some instances, rapid growth may

TABLE 6.1 GROWTH OF INDUSTRIAL PRODUCTION
(index, 1980 = 100)

Country	1981	1982	1983	1984	1985	1986	Growth rate 1980–86
Austria	98.4	97.6	98.5	103.8	108.4	109.9	1.9
Belgium	97.4	97.4	99.3	102.2	104.1	108.1	1.5
Denmark	—	—	—	—	—	—	—
Finland	102.9	103.8	107.1	112.1	116.5	117.5	2.9
France	99.0	97.0	98.0	100.0	101.1	102.0	0.5
Greece	99.3	94.9	94.3	97.3	107.2	109.1	1.6
Ireland	102.3	102.6	109.2	125.1	128.0	130.8	5.3
Italy	98.4	95.4	92.3	95.4	96.5	99.2	−0.2
Netherlands	98.0	94.0	96.0	101.0	104.0	106.0	1.3
Norway	99.0	99.0	107.0	113.0	117.0	122.0	3.9
Portugal	100.5	105.1	106.8	106.7	111.1	115.5	2.3
Spain	99.0	97.8	100.5	101.4	103.5	106.9	1.2
Sweden[a]	98.0	97.0	101.0	107.0	109.0	110.0	2.2
Switzerland	99.0	96.0	95.0	97.0	103.0	108.0	1.2
United Kingdom	96.6	98.4	101.9	103.2	108.1	109.6	2.0
West Germany	98.5	95.6	96.3	99.6	105.0	107.1	1.3
Western Europe	98.5	96.9	98.0	100.6	104.1	106.2	1.2

Source: ECE
[a] Includes mining and manufacturing only

give rise to particular types of structural change but in other cases flexibility and a rapid pace of structural change will help to ensure high rates of growth. Table 6.2 (p96) draws together data showing the structure of manufacturing value added in West Europe. The cluster of industries producing machinery and transport equipment (including automobiles) are among the most important in almost all countries. And with the exception of Greece and Portugal, the share of these industries in total MVA rose in all countries between 1970 and 1984. The relative growth of chemicals is another region-wide feature. Of the sixteen countries shown in Table 6.2 (p96), the share of chemicals rose in fourteen instances and was unchanged in the two remaining countries. A major field of contraction has been the textiles and clothing industries. The relative decline of these industries has been exceptionally large in Austria, Belgium and Ireland. Italy, one of the world's major exporters of high fashion clothing, was one of only two countries (along with Greece) where the industry's share of MVA has not declined. Finally, the share of food and agro-related industries in total manufacturing has changed

TABLE 6.2 COMPOSITION^a OF MANUFACTURING VALUE ADDED (as a percentage of total MVA)

	Food and agriculture		Textiles and clothing		Machinery and transport equipment		Chemicals		Other manufacturing	
	1970	1984	1970	1984	1970	1984	1970	1984	1970	1984
Austria	15	15	12	8	21	24	5	7	47	46
Belgium	16	19	13	8	24	25	10	13	37	35
Denmark	21	22	7	5	23	24	6	8	43	41
Finland	13	10	9	7	18	24	5	6	55	53
France	16	17	10	7	29	34	10	10	36	32
Greece	21	20	21	21	14	11	6	8	39	39
Ireland	34	32	19	10	12	18	5	15	30	25
Italy	10	12	18	18	24	26	8	8	40	37
Netherlands	16	19	8	4	27	28	11	13	38	37
Norway	15	10	6	3	27	28	5	8	47	51
Portugal	16	16	32	30	12	10	5	8	35	37
Spain	8	14	22	16	24	19	8	8	39	44
Sweden	9	9	6	3	28	33	5	7	52	49
Switzerland	12	14	9	8	26	25	8	12	45	41
United Kingdom	11	13	8	7	34	34	7	11	39	36
West Germany	10	10	8	5	37	44	8	9	38	32
Average (unweighted)	15.2	15.8	13.0	10.0	23.8	25.4	7.0	9.4	41.3	39.7

Source: World Bank
^a The definition of manufacturing groups is based on the following classification of the ISIC: food and agriculture (ISIC 311, 313 and 314), textiles and clothing (ISIC 321–24), machinery and transport equipment (ISIC 382–84) and chemicals (ISIC 351 and 352). Other manufacturing comprises ISIC Major Division 3, less all of the above.

very little since 1970. The fact that income elasticities for these goods are low in comparison with those for other manufactures would mean that a long-term decline in this group's share of MVA could be expected. However, the generous levels of protection and subsidies which many West European governments provide – both to these industries and to their suppliers in the agricultural sector – have probably helped to avoid this fate.

With regard to structural change, the concept is generally taken to refer to shifts in the composition of manufacturing output. Ideally, such indicators would represent permanent rather than transitory changes in distribution of output. That is, they would exclude changes which are purely cyclical or temporary. But such a distinction is very difficult to maintain in practice. Summary measures of structural change for the entire manufacturing sector are shown in Table 6.3 (p98). Changes have been estimated on the basis of two-year averages between the years 1978–79, representing the peak of the previous cycle, and 1983–84, the two latest years in the current upswing for which comparable data are available. Because the figures inevitably include cyclical as well as secular trends, the results should be interpreted in conjunction with corresponding measures of consistency. The latter measure, which is derived from changes in the production patterns during each individual year in the period 1978–84, would take a value of unity when there have been no reversals in year-to-year changes in industry shares (i.e. a totally consistent pattern of change). A value of zero would mean that annual variations cancel out completely.

The results of this exercise show that the pace of structural change has been greatest in Norway, followed by Sweden and the United Kingdom. In the case of Norway, the magnitude of adjustment should be discounted to some extent since the measure of consistency indicates that year-to-year changes in compositon of manufacturing output were often in opposite directions. Countries where the pace of change has been comparatively slow include Greece, the Netherlands, West Germany and Italy. A more complete impression of the extent of change throughout West Europe emerges when these results are compared with similar indicators for previous years. ECE estimates of the overall pace of structural change in West Europe for the period 1970–78 yield an average index of 5.70, albeit with a comparatively low measure of consistency (31 per cent). When judged against this benchmark,

TABLE 6.3   SUMMARY MEASURES OF STRUCTURAL CHANGE IN TOTAL
MANUFACTURING OUTPUT

Country	Index of structural change[a] 1978-79 to 1982-84	Measure of consistency[b]
Austria	2.80	0.4131
Belgium	3.89	0.8076
Denmark	4.00	0.5705
Finland	4.16	0.4851
France	4.16	0.5405
Greece	1.88	0.4045
Ireland	4.48	0.5199
Italy	2.60	0.3935
Netherlands	2.33	0.5673
Norway	7.52	0.4949
Portugal	3.61	0.4214
Spain	3.48	0.4936
Sweden	5.92	0.7262
United Kingdom	5.34	0.7407
West Germany	2.41	0.5452

Source: UN, UNIDO and author's calculations
[a] The measure of structural change (C) used here is defined as $C = \frac{1}{2} | a_{i2} - a_{i1} |$
   where a refers to the share of each industry in total manufacturing value added at
   current prices and $i = 1, \ldots, 28$. Period 1 represents a two-year average for 1978-79
   and period 2 refers to 1983-84
[b] The measure of consistency is defined as C divided by the sum of year-to-year
   changes (in percentage points) throughout the period 1978-84.

there are grounds to conclude that the pace of change has actually
slowed since the last peak of the economic cycle. During 1979–84,
very few countries recorded an overall rate of change that would
approach the earlier average. Such a feature can hardly be seen as
encouraging. Given the turbulence and rapidity of change in world
industry, the need for structural adjustment in West Europe would
have grown, while the opposite result appears to have occurred.

   An alternative view of structural patterns is obtained by considering the relative degree of specialization within the manufacturing
sector of each country. This approach amounts to a comparison of
each industry's share in total MVA in a particular country to the
unweighted average percentage share of the same industry in all
West European countries. When the ratio is substantially greater
than 100, the industry can be regarded as a field of specialization for
the country concerned; when it is substantially less than 100, the
industry is described as being 'under-represented'.

The relative degree of specialization was calculated for a total of fifteen industries in each of the sixteen West European countries. The industries chosen fall into three broad categories: light industries (mainly consumer products), resource-based industries and capital goods. The results of the exercise are summarized in Table 6.4. The picture which emerges after identifying fields of specialization and under-representation is somewhat different from that conveyed by Table 6.2.

TABLE 6.4   RELATIVE DEGREE OF SPECIALIZATION[a]

Industry (ISIC)	Specialization[b]	Under-representation[c]
Agro-processing (31)	Denmark, Ireland	Italy, Sweden
Textiles (321)	Greece, Portugal	Finland, W. Germany, Netherlands, Norway, Sweden
Clothing and footwear (322 + 324)	Greece, Italy, Portugal	Netherlands, Norway, Sweden
Leather (323)	Greece, Italy, Portugal, Spain	Denmark, Netherlands, Norway, Sweden
Wood and wood products (33)	Austria, Finland, Norway Portugal, Sweden	France, Ireland
Paper and paper products (34)	Finland, Norway, Sweden	France, W. Germany, Greece
Chemicals (35 less 355)	–	–
Rubber (355)	France, Italy, Spain	Denmark, Finland, Netherlands, Norway
Non-metallic minerals (36)	Greece, Ireland, Portugal	Sweden
Iron and steel (371)	Austria, Belgium, W. Germany, Spain	Denmark, Ireland
Non-ferrous metals (372)	Greece, Norway	Denmark, Portugal
Fabricated metal products (381)	Austria	–
Non-electrical machinery (382)	France	W. Germany, Portugal
Electrical machinery (383)	W. Germany, Netherlands	–
Transport equipment (384)	France, W. Germany, Sweden	Ireland

Source: UN, UNIDO and author's calculations
[a] Value added data were used to determine specialization. The measure is defined as the percentage share of each industry group in total MVA divided by the un-weighted percentage share of the same industry group for all West European countries. All percentages are using averages for 1983–84
[b] Specialization is defined to be a coefficient of 140 or more
[c] Under-representation is defined to be a coefficient of 60 or less

With regard to light industries, agro-processing activities are a field of specialization for only two countries – Denmark and Portugal. The first of these countries is a major exporter of processed food items while the industry's prominence in the second case is mainly due to the country's comparatively incomplete industrial base. The textile industry, which is generally regarded as a heavy user of cheap, unskilled labour, features only in Greece and Portugal. Similar input characteristics would apply to much of the clothing, footwear and leather industries and the same two countries again have a high degree of specialization. Italy, too, is specialized in these fields although that fact can be mainly attributed to success in a higher fashion end of the product lines.

Resources are important for specialization in the wood and paper industries with obvious inter-industry links between the two. Although the shares of West European producers in total forest-product exports have generally declined as new producing countries have emerged, Scandinavian countries in particular remain rich in trees and the industry's long-term prospects are reasonably good. Finland, for example, accounts for one-seventh of the world's exports of paper and board products. In addition to abundant resources, relatively low wages are a major reason for the industry's prominence in Finland while cheap energy costs are important for Norwegian and Swedish firms. Together, the heavily-forested Scandinavian countries specialize in the provision of bulk paper products to the rest of Europe. Portugal is a relatively new entrant to parts of this industry. Its production of pulp (where wood accounts for up to one-half the cost) relies on tropical eucalyptus trees which grow seven times faster than nordic pine.

Among other resource-based industries, the chemical industry appears as a special case. Although the industry was shown to have grown more rapidly than total manufacturing, West Europe is heavily dependent on the Middle East for its supplies of naphtha and other essential inputs. Because of price rises, up to 20 per cent of European capacity for ethylene, polyethylene, polyvinyl chloride and related products was scrapped in 1980–84. To a large extent the degree of specialization has become a matter of government policy. Because publicly-owned firms have been slowest to rationalize, their share of European production has risen from 25 per cent in 1975 to 40 per cent in 1985. With regard to heavy industries, the degree of specialization is especially wide for steel as six of the fifteen West

European countries have a pattern which lies outside the selected norms. Few European steel producers are profitable. Moreover, decisions regarding levels of output and production capacity are partly based on political considerations rather than being subject to purely economic determinants.

Similar circumstances are found in the transport industry where European governments have traditionally come to the aid of loss-making automobile firms. Some producers, notably BMW and Volvo, are known for specializing in particular market segments. Several, however, have preferred to retain a wide range of models and, as a result, are often burdened with excess capacity and recurrent losses. In the production of non-electrical machinery, which includes machine tools, metal and wood-working machinery as well as much office equipment, only France can claim a significant degree of specialization. Surprisingly, these activities are under-represented in West Germany. This situation is reversed in the case of electrical machinery. West Germany and the Netherlands – where the industry is dominated by Philips – hold a substantial lead over their European rivals.

II Energy resources and price trends

In resource-poor economies such as most of those in West Europe, industries rely heavily on foreign suppliers for their raw materials and are especially sensitive to disruptions in the world markets for those commodities. Events in international oil markets have completely overshadowed developments in the markets for other natural resources. Oil prices in 1986 averaged $14.30, down from $27.50 in the previous year. In response to the price change, European industries have switched from gas to oil whenever possible. A further substitution is unlikely in 1987 – even if the price of oil should continue to decline. In comparison with their American counterparts, relatively few European firms outside the power-generating industry have such flexibility.

Until the late 1970s, European energy planners had operated on the assumption that a close link existed between changes in total industrial output and levels of energy consumption by industry. For example, the estimates in Figure 6.1 (p102) show that in 1973 the energy intensity ratio (defined as the tonnes of oil consumed per

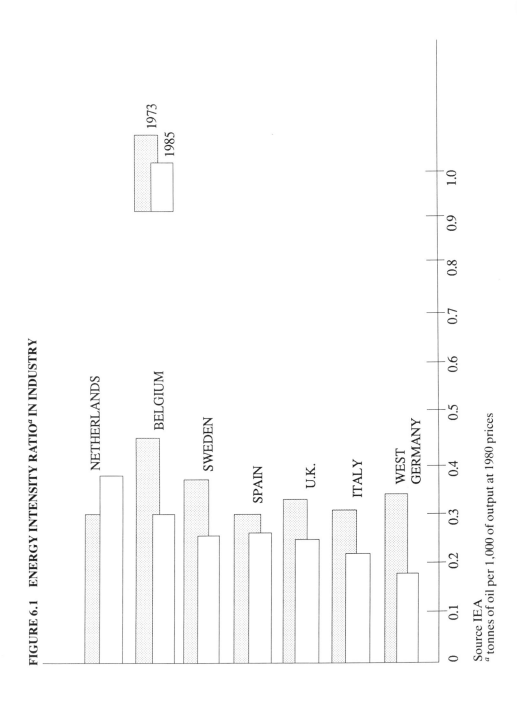

FIGURE 6.1 ENERGY INTENSITY RATIO^a IN INDUSTRY

1973
1985

NETHERLANDS

BELGIUM

SWEDEN

SPAIN

U.K.

ITALY

WEST
GERMANY

Source IEA
^{a} tonnes of oil per 1,000 of output at 1980 prices

$1000 of output at 1980 prices) ranged from 0.33 to 0.45 in West Europe. By 1985, the range of estimates had widened from 0.18 to 0.38. The general trend was also downward, suggesting that the link between industrial growth and energy consumption has been partially severed. Of the seven countries for which data are available, the energy intensity ratio has fallen everywhere except the Netherlands. The decline was significant in Belgium and West Germany and moderate in most other countries.

Three factors help to explain the gradual weakening of the long-standing relationship between industrial growth and energy consumption. They include the effects of energy conservation programmes, the impact of the economic slowdown and a move out of energy-intensive industries. While the first two of these effects have received considerable attention, the important role played by the last of these factors is not always recognized. Until very recently, the backbone of Europe's industrial growth has been a nucleus of industries such as steel, chemicals and automobiles, all of which were relatively heavy users of energy. By the late 1970s the growth impetus provided by these industries had begun to wane. New growth industries such as telecommunications, computers, semi-conductors and related components emerged instead. Unlike their predecessors, the leading industries of today are not such intensive users of energy. The effects of these industry-specific shifts were reinforced by more broadly based changes in economic structure. For instance, economy-wide shifts in the share of GDP have included the growth of services relative to the production of material goods. Because services are less energy intensive than industry, the link between the growth of GDP and energy usage was further eroded.

With regard to patterns of energy consumption among industries within manufacturing, the quality of available data is poor. Owing to such considerations, only tentative impressions of broad trends are possible. Table 6.5 (p104) indicates patterns of consumption in Western European industries in the mid-1980s for two major forms of energy – electricity and gaseous fuels. More fragmented evidence for earlier years in the 1980s (not shown) suggest a widespread decline in the rate of usage for both these energy sources. However, rates of consumption generally began to rise by 1984, implying that a portion of the reduction in previous years was due to the economic slowdown and not improvements in efficiency.

TABLE 6.5 CONSUMPTION OF ELECTRICITY AND GASEOUS FUELS BY INDUSTRY

Countries	Consumption pattern for electricity in total industry,[a] 1984 (percentage)					Consumption pattern of gaseous fuels in total industry[a] and construction, 1985 (percentage)			
	Total manufacturing (ISIC 3)	Food, beverages and tobacco (ISIC 31)	Textiles, wearing apparel, leather products (ISIC 32)	Chemicals, petroleum, coal, rubber and plastic products (ISIC 35)	Basic metal industries (ISIC 37)	Food, beverages and tobacco (ISIC 31)	Textiles, wearing apparel, leather products (ISIC 32)	Chemicals, petroleum, coal, rubber and plastic products (ISIC 35)	Basic metal industries (ISIC 37)
Belgium[b]	83.2	6.8	3.9	30.4	21.3	3.1	1.4	23.6	46.2
Denmark[b d]	99.3	26.7	3.4	20.1	9.8	—	—	—	—
Finland	87.5	3.5	1.4	12.3	9.2	—	—	—	—
France[c]	77.5	8.1	2.5[e]	20.7	17.6	2.0	1.3	25.2	19.9
Italy[b d]	94.4	5.8	7.4	25.1	23.3	6.9	4.4	19.1	25.9
Netherlands	90.0	10.9	1.4	38.5	23.8	13.2	1.6	53.2	7.8
Norway	98.0	4.2	0.4	16.4	55.7	—	—	—	—
Portugal	—	—	—	—	—	5.3	1.4	2.1	35.8
Spain[b]	81.4	7.5	4.0	17.9	25.3	3.6	5.4	21.1	43.7
Sweden[b]	77.4	3.6	0.7	12.0	14.6	8.2	0.9	7.8	62.8
Switzerland	—	—	—	—	—	12.8	3.4	38.8	4.3
United Kingdom	74.6	7.4	2.9	19.9	13.6	9.0	2.5	32.8	18.2
West Germany	81.6	4.1	2.4	27.8	20.5	5.6	2.4	27.9	40.0

Source: For electricity UN; for gaseous fuels ECE
[a] Total industry includes mining, manufacturing, electricity and gas industries (ISIC 2–4). [b] Electricity data refer to 1982. [c] Electricity data refer to 1982. [d] Data for gaseous fuels refer to 1984. [e] Only textiles (ISIC 321)

Within industry, manufacturing activities clearly account for a predominant portion of electricity usage. Similar estimates are not available for consumption of gaseous fuels although the same relationship is expected to exist for that energy source. The textiles, wearing apparel and leather industries are relatively unimportant users of energy while food, beverages and tobacco account for a moderate portion of the sector-wide total. Chemicals and related products (e.g. petroleum, coal-based products, rubber and plastic products) claim a much larger portion of the energy consumed by manufacturing. Likewise, the production of basic metals can be a relatively large consumer of energy in countries with a moderately large industrial and sufficient domestic resource endowments. The energy intensity of this last group – which consists of the steel and non-ferrous metals – is seen to be exceptionally high when compared with those industries' share of total manufacturing output. The relative contraction in the size of these activities would have been an important reason for the overall decline in energy consumption by manufacturing.

The prices of primary commodities other than energy weakened considerably in 1986. After reaching a peak in mid-1984, the HWWA (Hamburg) index of non-energy commodities fell by 10 per cent in 1985. At that point the index was roughly 30 per cent below its record level in 1980. The downward trend accelerated in 1986 as the dollar-based index fell by another 27 per cent. International markets for non-oil commodities continue to be characterized by conditions of oversupply and weak demand. A major reason is that, unlike previous recoveries, the present one has been dominated by the USA which is not as important an importer of primary products as Western Europe. In addition to the weakness of the current economic recovery, the demand for non-oil commodities is due to many of the same structural and technological factors which have depressed the demand for oil. These include a shift of output towards services and industries which are not resource-intensive along with technological changes which have reduced the raw material content of output.

III   Capital investment in industry

Information to assess patterns of capital investment in industry is often incomplete and marred by various conceptual difficulties. The most widely available source of data by type of industry concerns gross fixed capital formation. Although useful in obtaining an impression of year-to-year changes in investment, the short time period for which most of these series exist prevents the construction of a clear picture of cumulated investment on capital stock. Instead, the data represent different proportions of capital stock in different countries and time periods. Such indicators also give greater weight to investment in plant, machinery and transport equipment than to buildings, since the former have shorter lives. This feature, however, is not necessarily a defect since investment in plant and machinery can be expected to have a more direct bearing on production efficiency in industry than does investment in buildings.

Table 6.6 shows the growth of gross fixed capital formation for total industry along with a partial breakdown of these flows for investment in specific sub-sectors. With very few exceptions, rates of investment declined in 1981 over the previous year. Performance worsened in 1982 and 1983 as disinvestment occurred in at least one of those years in six of the eleven countries with available data. Investment continued to lag in 1984 in the United Kingdom and West Germany although it appeared to recover in several of the smaller countries.

The manufacturing sector tends to absorb the bulk of investment in industry. Norway is the only exception to this pattern and that result can be attributed to the heavy capital demands associated with the build-up of the country's offshore oil industry – an activity falling outside the manufacturing sector. Information on investment in specific industries within manufacturing is available for only four groups. The combined shares of these groups seldom accounted for as much as one-half of total gross capital formation for all manufacturing, a fact that would imply a fairly wide dispersement of investment pattern across a range of industries. Of the industry groups shown, chemicals has tended to be the largest recipient of investment funds although the share of food-related industries rose also moderately in several countries. Perhaps the most significant feature is the unimportance of basic metal industries which are known to be relatively capital intensive. Here, the low share can be attributed to the existence of considerable excess capacity and the efforts of many West European governments to reduce production capacity in the steel industry.

TABLE 6.6 GROSS FIXED CAPITAL FORMATION IN INDUSTRY

Countries	Annual rates of growth for total industry (ISIC 2–4)					Total manu-facturing (ISIC 3)	Shares in total industry, 1984 (percentage)			
	1980	1981	1982	1983	1984		Food, beverages and tobacco (ISIC 31)	Textiles, wearing apparel, leather products (ISIC 32)	Chemicals, petroleum, coal, rubber and plastic products (ISIC 35)	Basic metal industries (ISIC 37)
Austria[a]	12.5	13.0	-2.4	-7.4	—	62.2	8.9	4.3	8.1	5.6
Denmark[b]	15.2	-4.6	3.8	7.4	35.9	99.3	25.0	4.8	19.9	1.3
Finland	37.6	3.3	19.4	-6.1	7.7	76.8	7.9	2.2	11.1	3.0
France	20.9	5.1	8.4	4.7	8.6	70.7[c]	12.5	3.1	12.4[d]	6.5[e]
Ireland[a]	5.7	11.7	19.6	-20.4	—	57.9	21.1	2.4	8.3	0.3
Italy[f]	29.0	19.5	9.7	—	—	68.3	6.7	6.0	12.2	7.8
Netherlands	18.1	-8.5	-4.4	2.6	26.9	73.7	12.8	1.6	27.4	4.1
Norway	11.1	66.4	-23.7	10.3	46.6	19.1	4.0	0.2	2.6	2.8
Spain[a]	—	—	—	—	—	45.8	9.0	3.1	8.7	4.3
Sweden	26.5	10.0	0.1	14.0	12.6	66.4	6.0	1.1	8.8	3.9
United Kingdom	8.0	-0.8	7.3	-1.0	1.4	62.1	9.6	2.6	14.1	2.7
West Germany[g]	16.3	-0.2	1.7	3.2	0.3	70.6	7.3	2.6	13.5	4.9

Source: UN
[a] Shares in total industry refer to 1983
[b] Excl. electricity, gas etc. (ISIC 4)
[c] Incl. mining (ISIC 2)
[d] Incl. petroleum and gas (ISIC 220), excl. petroleum and coal products (ISIC 354)
[e] Incl. metal ore mining (ISIC 230)
[f] 1982
[g] Excl. prefabricated building parts and structures

IV   Industrial outlook

The inability of manufacturers in various fields such as steel and shipbuilding to fashion a response to slumping demand and intensified foreign competition has contributed to the atmosphere of industrial crisis in West Europe. One consequence is that appeals for new forms of industrial policy have moved to the forefront of discussion in many countries. These appeals are based on a variety of objectives – wish to facilitate the process of structural change, to accelerate the development and application of advanced technologies or, more generally, to boost the productive potential of industry.

Though industrial policies will vary greatly from country to country, there are several reasons to expect an increase in the frequency of government intervention in West Europe over the next several years. First, in most countries industry accounts for a predominant share of tradable goods and export earnings. The significance of this relationship is accentuated by the prominent role of trade in all West European countries. Second, the pressure on governments to redress their unemployment problem is mounting. However, growth of employment in services has remained slow and authorities are now more sceptical about the potential employment benefits. There is also growing evidence that manufacturing and services are to a great extent complementary rather than competitive. These circumstances would imply that in the future public authorities will pay much greater attention to the employment-generating role of industry. Third, industry has strong links with other parts of the economy, making it an 'engine of growth' with spillover effects for other sectors. All these facts suggest that the sector will absorb the attention of policy makers to a greater extent than it has in the past with the result that government intervention will become even more common in the last years of this decade.

The outlook for growth in industrial output during this critical period is not bright. Industrial growth flattened out in the second half of 1986. Grounds for pessimism should be tempered, however, as regional figures conceal a revival of activity in specific countries and fields of industry. For example, there is fragmented evidence of a recent acceleration of total investment in manufacturing. After years of weak growth, the rise in investment holds promise for some improvement in the pace of industrial activity. Today, there are only three countries, Italy, the United Kingdom and Sweden where real investment levels are below those of 1973. The potential benefits of this recovery must, nevertheless, be viewed cautiously. Though the resumption of manufacturing investment has been brisk, the long-term trend for 1973–86 remains well below the rate in earlier periods. This means that a sizeable portion of the present investment surge is for replacement. In fact, in Belgium, France, Finland, the Netherlands and Sweden 50 to 60 per cent of all gross fixed capital investment in manufacturing during 1984–86 is thought to have been for replacement of capital goods.

The slump has been mainly confined to the four largest West European countries; in several of the smaller economies industrial production has picked up. Despite these qualifications, the region's prospects for industrial growth are not bright and have been scaled back during the first half of 1987.

CHAPTER SEVEN
EXTERNAL TRADE FLOWS AND PATTERNS

The significant role played by international trade in all West European economies has already been noted. Although the region's share in world trade has declined slowly since the early 1970s, Western European countries still accounted for nearly two-fifths of the global total in 1985. This chapter examines some of the more important features of West Europe's trade patterns. The discussion begins with a survey of recent trends in the balance of payments. This is followed by an assessment of export performance. The subsequent material highlights two prominent features of Western European trade, the growing role of invisible exports and the overwhelming importance of intra-European trade. The chapter concludes with a survey of import trends and trade restraints.

I Balance of payments

Recent developments in the current account position of Western European countries have mirrored changes in the trade and current account of the USA. Although the USA reported a surplus on its current account as recently as 1981, its deficit in 1986 was $140 billion, making it the world's largest debtor. The dramatic shift in the US payments position was a major reason for the general improvement in the accounts of most Western European countries. The current account position of Western European countries has also benefited from an improvement in the terms of trade owing to a fall in commodity prices – in particular, the decline in oil prices.

Table 7.1 shows the current account position of West European countries in the 1980s. The region's combined account steadily

TABLE 7.1 CURRENT ACCOUNT BALANCES[a]

	Current account balance (in millions of US dollars)					Current account balance (as a share of GDP)				
	1981	1982	1983	1984	1985	1981	1982	1983	1984	1985
Austria	-1464	641	177	-626	-262	-2.0	1.1	0.6	-0.3	-0.1
Belgium[b]	-4174	-2616	-431	—	250	-4.6	-3.3	-0.5	-0.4	0.5
Denmark	-1875	-2259	-1176	-1637	-2728	-3.0	-4.2	-2.6	-3.3	-4.4
Finland	-373	-753	-936	5	-677	-0.8	-1.6	-1.9	—	-1.4
France	-4811	-12082	-5166	-876	1000	-1.4	-3.0	-1.7	-0.8	-0.8
Greece	-2408	-1892	-1878	-2132	-3000	-6.5	-4.4	-5.1	-4.1	-8.3
Ireland	-2611	-1905	-1202	-922	-500	-14.7	-10.6	-7.0	-6.1	-3.8
Italy	-8604	-5684	555	-287	-7500	-2.3	-1.6	0.2	-0.9	-1.2
Netherlands	2906	3700	3859	5158	5350	2.2	3.2	3.1	4.1	4.3
Norway	2177	662	1986	2976	2926	3.8	1.1	3.6	5.4	5.1
Portugal	-2605	-3250	-1004	-514	-100	-11.8	-12.7	-6.3	-1.9	3.0
Spain	-4989	-4245	-2746	231	2600	-2.7	-2.5	-1.5	1.3	1.7
Sweden	-2847	-3526	-923	374	-1016	-2.5	-3.6	-1.0	0.4	-1.2
Switzerland	1498	3934	1197	4019	3500	2.9	4.1	4.0	4.8	5.6
United Kingdom	13059	6872	4730	1928	5341	2.3	1.2	0.7	-0.3	1.0
West Germany	-5030	3926	4219	6770	13768	-0.8	0.5	0.6	1.0	2.2
Total/average share (unweighted)	-22151	-18477	1261	13963	18952	-2.6	-2.3	-0.9	-0.1	0.1

Source: When possible, data for current account balances were taken from the IMF. Preliminary estimates for 1985 were taken in some cases from ECE. Figures on shares were derived from OECD data
[a] Excludes exceptional financing
[b] Includes Luxembourg

improved during the period, moving from a deficit in 1981 and 1982 to a surplus in later years. By 1985, West Europe had a combined surplus of $19 billion, up from $14 billion in the preceding year. Changes in the current account position of the region have been dominated by circumstances in West Germany. That country's current account moved into surplus in 1982 and has grown in each subsequent year. This trend was originally due to a decline in net payments on services and investment income. In more recent years steady improvements in the West German trade balance have led to even larger current account surpluses. By 1985, the West German figure exceeded $13 billion, equivalent to more than 70 per cent of the total European surplus. Other countries showing an improvement in their current account position during the 1980s include Norway, Spain, Switzerland and the United Kingdom (in part, owing to the ending of the miners' strike). Elsewhere in West Europe, there was little improvement in the external position. For instance, the current accounts of many of the other smaller countries were persistently in deficit during the first half of the 1980s. Greece, Ireland and Denmark all recorded deficits which were between 4 and 7 per cent of GDP in most of these years.

Preliminary data for 1986 are shown in Figure 7.1. The estimates, which indicate the current account balance as a share of GDP, reveal some significant shifts in comparison with trends in the first half of the 1980s. Favourable trends in commodity prices and rapid growth in the balance for services have had a positive impact on the current accounts of several countries. These factors helped to reverse the current account position in Italy, resulting in a surplus equivalent to roughly one per cent of GDP. The same factors led to a modest improvement in that of France and further boosted the surplus of West Germany, which is estimated to be nearly 4 per cent of GDP for 1986. However, the fall in oil prices had an opposite effect for Norway and the United Kingdom – two of West Europe's oil producers. By 1986, Norway's current account was negative, amounting to more than 6 per cent of GDP, while the current account surplus in the United Kingdom was virtually erased.

II Export performance

The value of West European exports rose by 6 per cent in 1985. In

FIGURE 7.1 CURRENT ACCOUNT BALANCE, 1986

as % of GDP

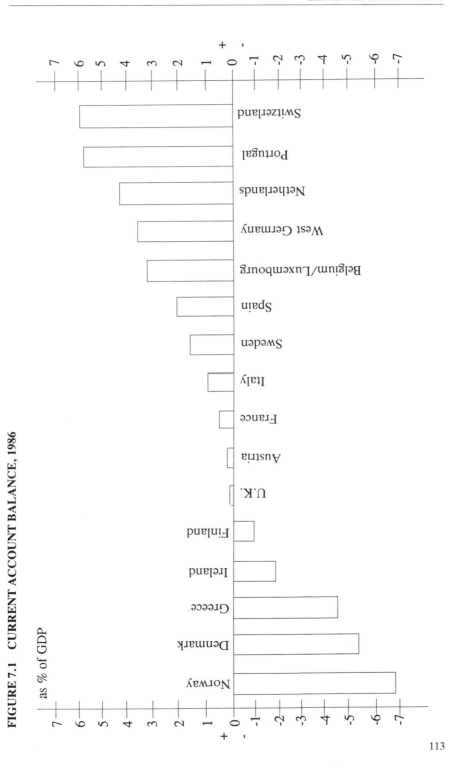

terms of volume, a slightly smaller increase (5.5. per cent) was recorded in that year. Table 7.2 shows the export drive was led by several of the region's largest countries, Italy, the United Kingdom and West Germany. Exports of each of these countries grew by more than 7 per cent in the year, a pace which was roughly the same as in 1984. Other countries which enjoyed an impressive growth in exports were Austria, Denmark and Ireland. Elsewhere, the growth of exports (in value) was generally lower than in the preceding year.

TABLE 7.2 EXPORT PERFORMANCE IN WEST EUROPE

	Exports, 1985 (bn US$)	Share in world exports, 1985 (percentages)	Growth rate in value, 1985 (percentage change over 1984)	Growth rate in volume, 1985 (percentage change over 1984)
West Germany	183.4	9.6	7.2	7.2
United Kingdom	101.1	5.3	7.2	7.1
France	97.4	5.1	4.6	3.0
Italy	79.0	4.1	7.6	6.0
Netherlands	68.3	3.6	3.7	4.0
Belgium[a]	53.3	2.8	3.7	4.0
Sweden	30.4	1.6	3.9	2.0
Switzerland	27.3	1.4	6.1	8.3
Spain	24.3	1.3	3.3	1.5
Norway	19.8	1.0	5.3	4.9
Austria	17.1	0.9	8.8	9.5
Denmark	16.4	0.9	6.3	4.4
Finland	13.6	0.7	0.8	4.0
Ireland	10.4	0.5	7.9	6.5
Portugal	5.2	0.3	0.9	8.5
Greece	4.5	0.2	−6.8	5.9

Source: GATT, ECE, UN and author's calculations
[a] Includes Luxembourg

Indirect information on the movement of export prices can be obtained by comparing the two sets of growth rates in Table 7.2. For instance, the figures for Finland and Portugal show that the value of exports rose negligibly in 1985 despite significant increases in export volume. Other countries where the growth in volume of exports exceeded gains in value include the Netherlands, Belgium and Austria. However, the widest discrepancy between the two rates of growth was in Greece where the value of exports declined by 7 per cent although volume rose by almost 6 per cent. More favourable price effects were enjoyed by exporters in France, Italy, Sweden, Spain and Denmark.

In addition to various forms of price and non-price competition, a country's trade performance depends on economic conditions in the markets it supplies and the dynamism of the goods which it exports. The first of these aspects, the direction of trade, has been examined in Chapter 1. Table 7.3 shows changes in the composition of West Europe's exports during the 1970s and 1980s. In broad terms, the changing composition of European exports represents a continuation of trends which have prevailed since the 1970s.

TABLE 7.3   WESTERN EUROPE'S MERCHANDISE EXPORTS
(INCLUDING INTRA-TRADE) BY PRODUCT GROUP
(percentage)

Total exports[a]	1973 100.0	1981 100.0	1985 100.0
Food	11.7	11.0	9.7
Fuels	3.7	9.4	9.3
Other primary products	7.8	6.0	5.5
Manufactures	75.8	72.2	73.9
of which:			
Chemicals	10.5	11.8	13.1
Iron and steel	6.4	5.1	4.6
Other semi-manufactures	6.9	6.4	6.3
Office and telecommunication equipment	3.1	3.0	4.5
Machinery for specialized industries	11.6	10.4	9.8
Road motor vehicles	8.5	8.1	8.4
Other machinery and transport equipment	12.5	13.0	12.8
Household appliances	3.1	2.3	2.4
Textiles	5.1	3.5	3.4
Clothing	2.4	2.2	2.3
Other consumer goods	5.7	6.1	6.2

Source: GATT
[a] Total exports include unspecified products

With regard to primary exports, the share of food and other non-fuel products has gradually declined. These goods accounted for less than 10 per cent of the region's total exports in 1985. Surprisingly, six of the world's major exporters of food in 1985 were members of the EC. Of these, West Germany, Italy, the United Kingdom and Belgium-Luxembourg significantly increased their respective shares of world exports in recent years, mainly at the expense of the USA and Australia. These gains have occurred at a time when world demand for many food products is stagnating, largely due to the unexpected growth of agricultural output in countries which previously satisfied most of their food needs through imports. In the case of oil, increased deliveries by Norway and the United Kingdom meant that the share of fuel in the region's exports remained fairly stable during the first half of the 1980s.

Primary products are of much less importance in West Europe's overall export pattern than are manufactures. The latter category accounts for almost three-fourths of the region's exports. Chemicals is one of only a few industries where the export share has shown a long-term rise. By 1985, chemicals claimed the largest share of West Europe's manufactured exports (13.1 per cent). As in the case of food products, the growing importance of chemicals may pose problems for the European industry. The emergence of many new (and lower cost) suppliers in the Middle East threatens to undercut many of the European industry's traditional export markets. The vast size of several schemes means that such a prospect must be taken seriously. Development of the huge Saudi Basic Industries Corporation (Sabic), for example, is expected to account for 4 per cent of the world's petrochemical supplies by the end of the 1980s. European multinationals are not represented in the project's many joint ventures and the disruptions to their markets may be significantly greater than those to be experienced by Japanese or American producers.

Aside from chemicals, the only other product categories to show a significant improvement in export performance were suppliers of various types of electronic products. The value of West Europe's exports of all electronic products was $42 billion in 1985, representing a 15 per cent increase over the previous year. The region's exports were nearly two-fifths of all OECD exports of these goods, making it the major supplier of electronic products. Within Europe, member countries of the EC are the dominant suppliers, accounting for 88 per cent of the region's total exports of electronic products in 1985.

Although world trade in electronic products decelerated abruptly in 1985 (due mainly to the slump in the USA), the strong performance by European exporters enabled several major producers to recover some of the market share lost in preceding years. The turnaround was mainly due to exports of computers and, to a lesser extent, telecommunications equipment and business electronics.

The region leads in the export of computers (more than $16 billion in 1985) although several of its producers are subsidiaries or affiliates in Japan and the USA. European firms were perhaps fortunate that markets for telecommunications equipment, a field in which they have a relative specialization, did not experience the sharp downturn in 1985 which occurred for most electronic products. These products accounted for 4.5 per cent of the region's manufactured exports in 1985, up from 3.1. per cent in 1973 (see Table 7.2). Finally, in the area of business electronics foreign sales of electronic control instruments by EC exporters have rebounded, amounting to $4.4 billion in 1985. The gains of European producers in this category helped to offset losses in related export markets, notably photocopying machines where Japanese suppliers made large inroads.

Export performance was far less impressive in other fields, notably steel. Together with Japan, West Europe accounts for more than three-fourths of world steel exports. Much of the region's exports are now covered by bilateral restraint agreements involving not only European steelmakers but others as well. Another reason for diminishing export prospects in the steel industry is the emergence of important new exporters such as Brazil and South Korea. Mainly owing to the establishment of such new capacity, West Europe's share of world steel exports has fallen by 7 per cent since 1979–1984. Table 7.3 shows the effects of these factors in terms of a long-term decline in the industry's share of total West European exports.

The share of motor vehicle exports (which consist almost entirely of passenger automobiles) has remained constant, accounting for roughly 8 per cent of the total throughout the period 1973–85. Of the three most successful exporters in the 1980s, West Germany and Spain recorded increases of more than 10 per cent in 1985. In Sweden, the third major exporter, growth slowed to 2.5 per cent in 1985 after an exceptional performance in 1984 when exports rose by 19 per cent. Three other producers – France, Italy and the United Kingdom – all lost market share as the value of their exports declined in 1985.

In the textile and clothing industries, Western Europe's share of world trade steadily declined in the period 1979–84. The downward trend was reversed in 1985 as European suppliers outperformed their rivals in East Asia and the USA. However, improvements were mainly the result of changes in the dollar value of the various region's exports. When expressed in national currencies, the growth of West Europe's exports of textiles and clothing was slower in 1985 than in 1984. The net result was that the share of these industries in West Europe's total exports merely stablilized in 1985 at proportions roughly equivalent to those in 1981.

III   Intra-European trade

While the foregoing discussion has considered West Europe's role in world trade, a large proportion of all exports do not leave the region. European buyers often account for as much as three-fourths of an industry's exports. Table 7.4 provides an overview of intra-European trade. The share of such trade in the region's total exports is shown in the first column. Figures in the second column indicate the composition of intra-European trade while the growth of intra-regional trade is given in the final column.

In 1985, intra-regional trade accounted for more than two-thirds of all West European exports and 60 per cent of its manufactured exports. Although the proportion of intra-regional trade in non-manufactures is high, the significance of these products in the region's total exports is not great (see Table 7.3). Within manufactures, intra-regional trade accounts for at least one-half (and often much more) of West Europe's exports to the world in each category shown in Table 7.4. Intra-regional trade is an especially large portion of total exports in the textile and clothing industries, household appliances, office and telecommunication equipment and semi-manufactures.

Reasons for the preponderance of intra-regional trade are many. In addition to the advantage of low transport costs and market proximity, the effects of EC and EFTA trade policies are obvious. But there are also other, industry-specific reasons for the significance of intra-regional trade. One, the tendency for public procurement practices in West Europe to favour European suppliers, has provided a significant boost to intra-European trade in office and telecommunications equipment. The EC's trade policies, notably its steel pact with the USA and its participation in the Multifibre Agreement, have altered trading patterns in the steel,

TABLE 7.4   INTRA-EUROPEAN^a EXPORTS BY
MAJOR PRODUCT CATEGORY

	As a share of West Europe's world exports in each category, 1985 (%)	As a share of total intra-European trade, 1985 (%)	Change in intra-European trade 1984–85 (%)
Food	68.7	10.6	3.6
Fuels	82.4	12.0	1.9
Other primary products	74.4	6.4	−2.2
Manufactures	59.7	69.7	8.2
of which:			
Chemicals	61.7	12.7	6.6
Iron and steel	57.9	4.2	5.9
Other semi-manufactures	66.1	6.6	3.8
Office and telecommunication equipment	66.4	4.7	17.1
Machinery for specialized industries	49.4	7.7	12.8
Road motor vehicles	60.0	7.9	11.8
Other machinery and transport equipment	51.9	10.4	6.9
Household appliances	66.0	2.4	6.8
Textiles	72.2	3.9	6.4
Clothing	78.5	2.9	6.5
Other consumer goods	63.1	6.3	6.9
Total intra-European exports^b	63.4	100.0	6.2

Source: GATT and author's calculations
^{a} Figures include only countries in the EC and EFTA
^{b} Totals include unspecified products

textile and clothing industries in a similar way. Finally, the efforts of many non-European multinationals to 'move behind' Europe's trade barriers has meant that they developed new production capacity within the region to be used as an export platform for other West European markets.

Turning to the product composition of intra-regional trade, manufactures again dominate, accounting for 70 per cent of the total. Chemicals accounts for the largest portion of this trade, 12.7 per cent in 1985. Intra-European trade in machinery of various types and in motor vehicles is also large. Trade in fuels accounted for 12 per cent of all intra-European exchange in 1985 and has been rising during the 1980s as European buyers have shifted their dependence to 'more secure' suppliers in the region.

In comparison with West Europe's exports to other regions (see Table 1.9) the growth of intra-regional trade has been rapid. In 1985, markets in North America and Asia were the only ones where rates exceeded the growth of intra-regional trade (6.2 per cent). By this standard, manufactures have clearly outperformed non-manufactures. Intra-regional trade in office and telecommunications equipment, specialized machinery and motor vehicles all grew by impressive rates in 1985. Altogether, intra-European trade in manufactures expanded by 8.2 per cent, a rate far greater than the growth of exports to the rest of the world.

IV   Exports of invisibles

Largely at the initiative of the US government, the subject of trade in services has come to attain a more prominent position in the international policy agenda. Despite growing interest in the field, the detailed information needed to assess or monitor these trade flows is often lacking. Balance of payments statistics provide the most ready source of data for measuring exports of services, or invisibles. These flows, which are identified by type of activity, include both non-factor services (e.g. travel and transport) and factor services (royalties, investment income, etc.). Factor services, however, do not necessarily distinguish between income from goods-related investment and that from service-related investment. Another drawback is that workers' remittances are generally included under 'transfers' in the balance of payments though they are actually a component of factor services. The latter receipts are of considerable importance in the case of Portugal and moderately significant for Greece.[1]

Using a balance of payments approach, exports of invisibles are loosely pictured as consisting of four major categories: shipments, other transport and passenger services, travel and tourism and other private services. While the relative importance of each category varies, transport and passenger services along with other private

---

[1] Balance of payments data on services in West Europe are likely to understate actual trade. Some portion of trade in goods may actually be trade in services while data on various components (for example provider-located services such as education or medical care) may not be recorded at all.

services tend to be the two most important contributors to invisible exports in the majority of West European countries. In a lesser number of countries – notably Austria, Italy and Switzerland – travel and tourism is traditionally an important earner of foreign exchange while shipping figures prominently in the invisible exports of only a very few countries.

Table 7.5 shows the export patterns for invisibles during the period 1980–85. It is immediately apparent from these figures that

TABLE 7.5   GROWTH OF EARNINGS ON INVISIBLE EXPORTS[a]
(year-to-year change in percentage)

	1981	1982	1983	1984	1985
Austria	1.9	7.7	−1.3	−7.2	14.0
Belgium[b]	26.5	−0.6	−11.0	4.8	7.3
Denmark	5.8	−0.6	−0.8	5.4	10.1
Finland	20.3	1.7	−3.0	7.2	1.0
France	16.8	2.3	−7.8	4.2	6.4
Greece	14.7	−9.6	−15.7	0.3	−4.1
Ireland	0.6	3.4	−6.0	1.9	—
Italy	0.6	9.7	−0.4	7.8	7.0
Netherlands	5.9	4.3	−6.8	6.5	−6.3
Norway	17.4	−0.0	−8.3	5.5	12.2
Portugal	13.7	−18.5	−0.1	17.4	18.1
Spain	11.5	7.3	−1.7	14.4	5.6
Sweden	10.4	5.0	1.5	5.0	4.3
Switzerland	12.7	57.0	1.1	4.0	6.8
United Kingdom	31.0	5.9	−10.0	8.8	3.7
West Germany	5.7	9.9	−0.6	2.2	4.7
Total of above	16.2	5.6	−6.0	5.7	4.4

Source: IMF and author's calculations
[a] Includes earnings attributable to transport and travel, insurance and other non-factor services
[b] Includes Luxembourg

earnings from invisible exports tend to be much more volatile than other forms of trade. Receipts from invisible earnings were an important contributor to the region's combined balance of payment in 1981, growing at a rate of 16 per cent. They were of much less significance in subsequent years: invisible exports contracted in 1983 and grew only moderately in 1984 and 1985. Several countries – Belgium, Finland, France, Norway and the United Kingdom – recorded gains of more than 15 per cent in 1981 although the growth of earnings in 1982 slowed or even contracted in every case. By 1984, only two countries, Portugal and Spain, reported significant improvements in their earnings from invisibles. Shipping activities led to a boost in Norwegian exports in 1985 while earnings from tourism rose in Austria and Portugal.

Preliminary estimates for 1986 indicate that the region's combined earnings from invisible exports rose only slightly. Among the larger West European countries, improvements in the invisible exports of France and Italy made a valuable contribution to the current account surplus. Moderate gains were reported by the United Kingdom although these were not sufficient to offset deficits in other balance of payment components. In Greece, Portugal and Spain receipts from tourism and travel were relatively important components of invisible exports. Tourism alone accounts for up to one-fifth of current receipts in Spain. That country's net earnings in 1986 reached $10.2 billion, up from $7.1 billion in 1985. Portugal, too, enjoyed significant gains from tourism: receipts rose 40 per cent in 1986, although this result was partly a consequence of the depreciation of the dollar against West European currencies. Like Spain, the share of tourism in Greek revenues was approximately one-fifth of current receipts in the early 1980s but had fallen below 15 per cent by the middle of the decade.

Transfers from abroad – most of which are emigrants' remittances – are relatively important for Portugal and have recently risen in Greece, helping to compensate for the slow growth of tourism in the latter country. Emigrants' remittances are of less significance for Spain and have tended to fall in all countries during the 1980s. The downward trend may reflect a reduction, or at least stagnation, in the number of workers abroad. An additional reason is that the transfers have mainly affected West European currencies. When expressed in dollars, the downward trend reflected that currency's appreciation during 1979–84. The same currency effect would now help to explain why such transfers rose in 1986.

V   Imports and trade restraints

West Europe's growth of imports rose unexpectedly in the first three quarters of 1986. Import volume grew by nearly 7 per cent in that period compared with an increase of only 5.7 per cent for the entire year of 1985. The upsurge was partially due to fuel imports but manufactures, too, rose briskly. This development represents a modest departure from trends in the earlier part of the 1980s. In volume terms, imports expanded at a steady pace in 1983–85 but at a rate somewhat higher than the longer-term trend for the period since 1975. The recent acceleration in the growth of private consumption in many countries was one of the major reasons for the rise in imports.

Table 7.6 shows year-to-year changes in the volume of imports during 1984–86. In the latest year sizeable increases were reported by Belgium, Denmark, France, Portugal, Switzerland, the United Kingdom and West Germany. Though complete figures were not yet available for Spain, that country, too, had a substantial increase in 1986. In both the Iberian countries the rise in imports was the result not only of strong growth in domestic demand but also because of the removal of various import barriers which accompanied their membership in the EC.

TABLE 7.6   VOLUME OF MERCHANDISE IMPORTS
   (percentage change from previous year)

	1984	1985	1986[a]
Austria	8.6	5.6	4.7
Belgium-Luxembourg	5.3	4.0	10.9
Denmark	7.8	7.2	9.9
Finland	1.0	5.1	5.6[d]
France	2.3	4.1	7.4[b]
Greece	−0.1	4.0	—
Ireland	10.4	3.4	−1.1
Italy	9.0	8.8	7.3[c]
Netherlands	6.2	6.9	3.1
Norway	14.7	11.9	10.3[d]
Portugal	−3.2	1.5	14.5[e]
Spain	1.0	3.0	—
Sweden	3.9	9.3	3.9[d]
Switzerland	7.7	5.4	9.3[b]
United Kingdom	9.5	5.3	6.7[d]
West Germany	5.2	4.2	6.3[b]

Source: IMF, OECD and ECE
[a] Unless otherwise indicated, January – September
[b] January – November
[c] OECD estimate for full year
[d] Official estimate for full year
[e] ECE estimate

The growing volume of imports should be seen in conjunction with price trends. When expressed in dollar terms, unit values for West Europe's imports rose by as much as 15 per cent in 1986. They declined, however, when expressed in national currencies. Altogether, West Europe's terms of trade improved by roughly 10 per cent in the latest year with West Germany recording a rise of almost 17 per cent. Norway was one of the few exceptions to the upward movement in terms of trade. The deterioration in that country reflected its heavy dependence on oil exports rather than any significant rise in the price of its imports. The relative price movements for traded goods had important implications for trade balances. In fact, in the absence of such gains, trade balances would generally have deteriorated, since the volume of imports tended to increase much more rapidly than that of exports.

Table 7.7 shows the value of West Europe's merchandise imports (including intra-regional trade) in selected years. Because of the region's heavy reliance on foreign supplies of fuel, drastic movements in the price of oil have led to correspondingly wide swings in the structure of imports. Between 1973–81, the share of fuel in total imports more than doubled. This shift was accompanied by a fall in the shares of food, primary products, steel, specialized machinery and textiles. The share of fuels had declined by the mid-1980s as the price of oil dropped, while the proportion of chemicals and office machinery in total imports had grown.

Broad trends such as these cannot reflect many of the underlying tensions which arise in connection with trade imbalances and sometimes divide European countries or pit the region against other major trading partners. West Europe's involvement in the world trading system is much greater than that of the USA or even Japan. This fact, however, is not sufficient to explain the growing frequency of trade-related disputes which clutter international agendas. The reasons for such disputes are found not in West Europe's trade successes but in the protectionist nature of many of its major programmes.

With regard to intra-European trade, there are no longer any tariff or quota barriers between members of the EC. Nor are such measures applied to the trade of EFTA countries or even that between the two country groups. Nevertheless, there are many forms of import restraint which are a recurrent source of regional disagreement. Governments have replaced tariffs with a host of

TABLE 7.7   WESTERN EUROPEAN MERCHANDISE IMPORTS (INCLUDING
INTRA-TRADE) BY PRODUCT GROUP
(percentage shares)

	1973	1981	1985
Food	16.4	11.6	11.5
Fuels	11.2	24.8	19.1
Other primary products	12.8	8.5	8.1
Manufactures	58.9	54.0	60.1
Chemicals	8.3	9.0	10.3
Iron and steel	4.8	3.0	3.1
Other semi-manufactures	6.2	5.2	5.5
Machinery for specialized industries	7.6	5.9	5.8
Office and telecommunication equipment	3.0	3.3	5.3
Road motor vehicles	5.6	5.6	6.3
Other machinery and transport equipment	9.4	9.0	9.6
Textiles	4.2	2.9	3.2
Clothing	2.6	2.7	3.1
Other consumer goods	4.6	4.9	5.3
Total imports[a]	100.0	100.0	100.0

Source: GATT
[a] Total imports include unspecified products

non-tariff barriers (NTBs) that favour the home country's producers at the expense of other European suppliers. Tariff-free protection against imports demands ingenuity. Inspiration for creation of NTBs often derives from the lack of common industrial standards. The lack of any generally accepted body of standards applies not only for the region as a whole but is the source of import restraints between member countries of the EC and EFTA. West Germany, France, the United Kingdom and other countries each have their own agencies to set national manufacturing norms for reasons of efficiency, health, safety or other concerns. Although efforts to create an EC-wide set of standards have been attempted, the pace of product development has been too swift. By the time community-wide agreements had been reached, new national standards were already in place.

Methods of public procurement constitute a more subtle form of NTB which further limits intra-regional trade. Government purchases, including orders of military and space equipment, account for as much as 15 per cent of the EC's national income. These practices, however, remain a national preserve. Procurement practices in the United Kingdom are typical of most European countries. West

Germany was the major non-British recipient of government contracts in 1979–80 but obtained only 7 per cent of the total. No other EC country received more than 3 per cent of Britain's government purchases.

A key element in the Community's confrontations with the USA is its protectionist agricultural policies. The programme, known as the Common Agricultural Policy (CAP), consists of a complex set of price supports and other subsidies, which have brought the EC self-sufficiency in the production of many agricultural products. But as output surpassed European needs, some of the surpluses have been dumped on world markets. Because the USA has long been the world's major exporter of many of the same products, trade disputes and the threat of protectionist retaliation in other fields have clouded EC–US relations. European negotiators have countered that both the USA and Japan provide generous subsidies to their own farmers. The Community has also taken steps to scale back the CAP. However, these were mainly a response to the growing financial burden of the programme and not a reaction to international criticism. At a more fundamental level, many non-European observers are sceptical of the EC's ability to put together a set of agricultural reforms which will significantly reduce the likelihood of dumping these surpluses on world markets. Until this fact is achieved, there is a danger that the Community's trading partners will retaliate through protectionist measures of their own.

Another dimension of the protectionist dilemma concerns the Community's efforts to mount a protectionist response to Japan's practice of concentrating on selected sectors in order to build up a dominant position in world markets. Japanese successes have cost the EC severely in industries including shipbuilding, motorcycles, VCRs, portable televisions, photocopiers and others. To date, the European response has primarily been to fight a rear-guard action by claiming that the products are being dumped and threatening to impose penal duties. But in a move which has long been supported by the French, the Community has announced its intention to define an EC product. The definition could exclude products that are made by foreign-based multinationals and sold in Europe as well as products assembled in Europe but containing an excessive amount of 'foreign' components. Producers of cars, television sets and video equipment which are assembled from foreign (mainly Japanese) components would be especially hard hit by such a policy.

The ultimate threat of NTBs in whatever form is that they are highly communicable, spreading quickly from one foreign supplier to others. Voluntary export restraints or orderly marketing agreements, for example, may isolate the original supplier but the source of disruption is soon refocused. Relief from foreign competitors will be effective only for the period of time required for other suppliers to cash in on the premium price established in the restrained market. At the same time, the exporters which were the original target of the restraint often shift into related products in order to by-pass the agreement. The danger of communicability is that discriminatory agreements will eventually have to be generalized to cover entire industries such as steel, chemicals or semiconductors and involve all major suppliers.

CHAPTER EIGHT
THE EUROPEAN MARKET

I   Introduction

Private consumption in Europe accounts on average for rather more than half of the total gross domestic product, and the proportion has been growing since the mid-1970s as increasing levels of real spending power have combined with reduced government budgets to shift the macroeconomic emphasis more and more squarely on to the individual and his lifestyle.

The early 1980s have, of course, been dominated by the aftermath of the second oil price shock in 1979, whose effects have been percolating through all European countries. The rapid rise in fuel costs filtered through to the consumer by raising the real cost of manufacturing, by depressing industrial investment and thus the job market, and finally by forcing up the interest rates paid by consumers.

In 1987, however, it is clear that better times are on the way. Purchasing of consumer goods and services has responded well to the easing of the international environment which followed the recovery of the American market in 1983. Falling interest rates and de-regulated banking services have helped revive those areas of the durables market which have suffered most in the first part of the decade: cars, white goods and, to some extent, furnishings.

West Germany and (briefly but spectacularly) Norway have led the revival in the mid-1980s, with robust sales which have compensated on the whole for the negative effects of strong national currencies. But on the other hand, the crisis of the early 1980s has left an enduring mark on some other countries; stubborn unemployment, slow industrial investment and, worst of all, excessive foreign debt (especially in France, Belgium, Denmark, Portugal and

Greece) seem likely to depress the development of consumer markets until the end of the decade, and possibly beyond.

II Demographic trends and forecasts

The period since the Second World War has seen major fluctuations in the demographic balance between young and old, and to some extent between male and female, for most of the countries in Western Europe. The growing economic prosperity of the 1950s and 1960s was reflected in the almost universal 'baby boom' which saw the birth rate increase by up to 20 per cent during those years.

Generally speaking, males account for about 51.3 per cent of all live births, compared with the female proportion of 48.7 per cent. In most European countries, males outnumber females up to around 50 years, but in West Germany and Belgium females start to predominate from 45 onwards.

With the benefit of hindsight, we can see three main consequences of the post-war surge in the birth figures. Firstly, the rapidly growing demand for educational and health facilities imposed strains on national infrastructures of a kind which have not been seen either before or since, and it necessitated an expansion of state welfare systems, especially in northern Europe. Secondly, it generated an important shift in consumer purchasing patterns, as increasingly affluent parents bought for their increasingly numerous offspring. Thirdly, the 'baby boom' created a 'bulge' of persons currently aged 17–35. This has undeniably been a major contributor to youth unemployment in many European countries, but it has at least assured their immediate elders of an adequate workforce to support them when they retire; compare, for example, the situation in Finland, where the absence of a significant baby boom has contributed in the 1980s to a shortage of labour, high wage demands, and ultimately an even worse strain on the economy.

In the early 1970s the European baby boom stopped almost as suddenly as it had started in most countries. It is not, on the whole, entirely adequate to blame the world economic recession which resulted from the first oil price shock of 1973/74, because family size has historically been relatively resistant to such downward fluctuations – although, as already seen, it is ready enough to respond to upward trends.

TABLE 8.1   WEST EUROPEAN POPULATION DEVELOPMENT

Unit: millions	1980	1981	1982	1983	1984	1985
Austria	7.55	7.56	7.57	7.55	7.55	7.56
Belgium	9.84	9.84	9.85	9.86	9.87	9.87
Denmark	5.13	5.12	5.12	5.12	5.11	5.12
Finland	4.78	4.80	4.82	4.86	4.88	4.89
France	53.58	53.84	54.09	54.34	54.73	55.00
West Germany	61.56	61.68	61.64	61.42	61.30	61.30
Greece	9.63	9.70	9.78	9.85	9.87	9.89
Ireland	3.40	3.44	3.48	3.52	3.54	3.55
Italy	56.43	56.50	56.64	56.84	56.98	57.05
Luxembourg	0.37	0.37	0.37	0.37	0.36	0.36
Netherlands	13.97	14.21	14.29	14.34	14.39	14.42
Norway	4.09	4.10	4.12	4.13	4.14	4.15
Portugal	9.78	9.89	9.97	10.05	10.13	10.20
Spain	37.24	37.52	37.89	38.07	38.28	38.40
Sweden	8.32	8.32	8.33	8.33	8.34	8.34
Switzerland	6.36	6.38	6.40	6.42	6.44	6.46
United Kingdom	55.95	55.83	56.29	56.38	56.49	56.55
Total	347.98	349.10	350.65	351.45	352.40	353.11

Source: IMF/national statistics

The most obvious reason for the fall in birth rates was simply the spread of contraceptive techniques; this was less obviously the case in certain Roman Catholic countries (Spain, Portugal, Italy and Ireland), although only Ireland actually bans contraception. The legalization of abortion in most countries has also helped to depress the birth statistics since the mid-1970s, especially in northern Europe and in the countries of the Warsaw Pact.

Another important trend is seen in the tendency of West European women to bear their first children at a later age than, say, thirty years ago; French statistics show, for example, that the average age rose by nearly five years between the mid-1950s and the mid-1980s.

There are three main reasons why this should be happening, all connected with the growth of female employment. Firstly, the delay before starting a family gives the dual-income couple enough time to equip the home more or less completely in advance of the birth; secondly, in those countries where housing costs are high or where house purchase is the norm, it may make all the difference to the standard of housing which they eventually achieve; and thirdly, it permits today's better educated woman in many cases to lay down the foundations of a career which she may seek to develop as her family grows. This last is more noticeable in northern Europe (excluding Ireland) than in countries to the south.

Trends in central Europe and much of Scandinavia seem to refute the theory that falling birth rates are due to economic decline. On the contrary, it seems in these countries to be prosperity which has induced young parents to limit the size of their families to rather less than the size required for the maintenance of a stable demographic balance. Some of the implications of this are explored below.

For much of Europe, improving standards of medical care have prolonged the life expectation of national populations, especially in those countries where living standards have been highest in the 1970s and 1980s. In northern Europe, the average age at death has risen by around ten years since 1945, meaning that the pressures on the welfare states are starting to shift away from education and back toward health care and retirement benefits. It has, of course, also boosted the markets for medical products and services, and for certain leisure goods.

It seems almost paradoxical that this increasingly healthy and long-lived European population of elderly people should be retiring from their working careers at an earlier rather than a later age. On the one hand they are being permitted to stop work earlier than hitherto, mainly because an increasingly wealthy society regards it as unacceptable for the elderly to have to work for as long as was once the case; but on the other hand the pressures of unemployment have also helped to encourage earlier retirement, making it appeal to employers as a means of providing job opportunities at the lower end of the age scale – where, clearly, they are most urgently needed by those bringing up young families. In 1987, the average legal retirement age for males in Europe is 62 years, while women stop work at an average 58 years.

The cumulative effect of falling birth rates and lower death rates is, of course, an overall ageing of the mean population, which in some countries takes on a truly alarming aspect. West Germany, on current projections, will have lost 14.5 million of its 60 million inhabitants between 1985 and 2030, leaving 80.7 persons of over 60 years of age to depend on every 100 of working age (20–59 years) – compared, for example, with a figure of 38.5 in 1985 and a projected 47.2 in 2000. In 2000, then, the over-60s will represent 26 per cent of the population; a similar ratio is likely in Sweden, as the over-65s increase in numbers to represent 21 per cent of the population in 2000, up from an already high 17 per cent in 1984.

Austria will be more fortunate; the proportion of over-65s will increase from 14.3 per cent in 1985 to 18.1 per cent in 2015, while the ratio of under-20s will drop from 26.4 per cent to 21.2 per cent, leaving a relatively stable working-age population at around 60.7 per cent of the total.

Denmark, too, can point to a reasonably stable picture, despite a fairly steep fall in the under-10 population between 1980 and 1986, thanks to a strong secondary 'boom' in the late 1960s. France, which kept up its 'baby boom' until the mid-1970s, is expecting its ratio of over-65s to increase to only 14.9 per cent by 2010, from 12.4 per cent in 1985; it is also expecting only a slight slowing in the birth rate in the next twenty years.

From a demographic point of view, Ireland shows the strongest growth at present. The surge in birth rates has actually increased since the 1960s and the 1981 census showed that 55 per cent of the population was aged under 30; we should add, however, that high levels of unemployment have induced large numbers of the country's young people to emigrate since then.

Spain and Portugal have maintained relatively smooth birth rates since the 1950s, although both may be expected to increase amid the increasing prosperity of the late 1980s. Neither appears to have an impending problem of age imbalance at present. Greece, too, has a reasonably favourable age spread despite the exceptional longevity of both sexes.

Geographically, European populations have continued in the last 30 years to drift toward the urban centres. The trend is especially noticeable in Greece, Spain and Italy (where depopulation of the depressed southern regions has become a major political issue); but it is also observable in France, which expects by 2000 to have lost a quarter of the rural population recorded in 1980. In Norway and Sweden, special regional assistance is offered to keep the often isolated northern communities alive.

III   Personal income and expenditure

The late 1970s and the first half of the 1980s have seen major changes in the pattern of income and consumption in Western Europe. On the one hand, the impact of the 1979 oil price rises fed through to the workforce by increasing the already quite steep pressure on export markets, and by raising interest rates to levels where new investment became uneconomic; the ensuing industrial recession of 1981–1984 boosted unemployment to levels which had not been seen since the 1930s. But in most countries, on the other hand, wage deals continued to outstrip the rate of inflation by an average of around 1.5 per cent, regardless of the fact that industrial productivity was making no more than modest progress.

The result, viewed very broadly, has been a widening of the economic gap between the employed and the unemployed, right across Europe. Those countries with a highly-developed welfare state (notably Belgium, the Netherlands, Norway and Sweden) have attempted to bridge it by increasing social benefits to the low-paid and the unemployed, so as to boost spending power at the lower end of the market. But the enormous cost of such subsidies has put national budgets under severe pressure, and several (notably Greece, Portugal, Ireland and the United Kingdom) have had to back off and reduce expenditure, while others (Belgium, France, the Netherlands and West Germany) have created 'solidarity funds' for the unemployed or have sought to create employment by reducing statutory working hours and by encouraging job-sharing. Only Sweden and Norway have borne the full cost of income redistribution, but at the expense of steep progressive rates of personal taxation, which in turn have fed the inflationary spiral.

In some countries, the economic recession of the early 1980s took much longer to filter through than in Britain, one of the first to feel its effects. In many countries (Belgium, Italy, Greece, Portugal, Luxembourg and Spain), this was because wages were cushioned from inflation by minimum wage statutes or by national systems of wage indexation. Often, as with Belgium and the Netherlands, awards under these systems failed to take account of shrinking industrial markets, and eventually placed unsupportably high price tags on national exports. But even a belated appreciation of the problem was not enough to put things right; it took time and often bitter political controversy to install corrective measures, because of public resistance to what was perceived as a winding down of socially responsible policies. The consequences of this delay have been most painfully felt in Belgium, the Netherlands and Greece;

for Spain and Portugal, its effects have been cushioned since 1986 by the industrial benefits of belonging to the European Community.

Among the more developed European countries, real consumption has been growing most rapidly in Norway, Sweden and Finland and most slowly in Belgium, Italy the Netherlands and Ireland. Growth in West Germany, relatively restrained until 1985, has resumed its upward path in 1986–87. Among the less industrialized countries of southern Europe, Greece and Spain have made exceptional growth from a relatively low base in 1980, while Portugal has lurched erratically to an overall rise of nearly 45 per cent, having weathered a deep trough in 1982–1984. In Switzerland, Austria and Luxembourg, the three countries best insulated by booming service industries, the growth of consumption has not been without its minor hold-ups but has generally managed a reasonable increase.

TABLE 8.2 DEVELOPMENT OF REAL TOTAL CONSUMPTION, 1980–1985
(in national currencies at 1980 prices: measured against the consumer price index)

Total consumption		1980	1982	1984	1985	% change, 1980/1985
Austria	Sch	592190	612085	639966	652791	10.23
Belgium	Bfr	2235066	2224338	2227633	2266991	1.42
Denmark	Dkr	207013	211298	226540	228332	10.29
Finland	Fmk	99320	106437	115214	125998	26.86
France	Fr	1742700	1823083	1924261	1997229	14.60
West Germany	DM	803200	789596	813111	815325	1.50
Greece	Dr	1152869	1199793	1422372	1492555	29.46
Ireland	I£	5990	5872	5761	6497	8.47
Italy	L(bn)	212561	187274	236408	200600	−5.62
Luxembourg	Bfr	79072	81901	85328	88546	11.98
Netherlands	Fl	201010	193090	194296	198462	−1.26
Norway	Nkr	131773	134911	145949	160120	21.51
Portugal	Esc	848100	1013335	1124898	1228314	44.83
Spain	P	10189000	11519905	11698201	12090449	18.66
Sweden	Skr	264277	271695	284822	302366	14.41
Switzerland	Sfr	103235	103863	107432	109859	6.41
United Kingdom	£	135336	136168	147747	154114	13.87

Source: Euromonitor

IV The European household

Viewed as a whole, the domestic unit in Western Europe has been getting smaller over the last twenty years as general levels of affluence have risen. This is partly the result of the declining birth rate, of course, whose impact has been especially noticeable in northern Europe; but it owes at least as much to other demographic and economic shifts. Job mobility and the general move toward the urban centres have both been major factors in the breakdown of the larger, extended family-based household into the nuclear and subnuclear structures of the present day. The growth in the incidence of divorce since the 1960s has contributed to the number of small, often one-parent households seeking appropriately small-scale accommodation in the cities and elsewhere.

As Table 8.3 indicates, the number of dwellings per thousand inhabitants is surprisingly uniform in much of northern Europe, at around 400. Denmark, France and West Germany have the largest housing stock, all with particular emphasis on the major cities; Ireland, Greece and Portugal appear to maintain the largest household units, with an average 3.7 persons in each dwelling.

TABLE 8.3 EUROPEAN HOUSING, 1985

	Number of dwellings ('000)	Dwellings per '000 inhabitants	Household size (1984/85)	One-person households (% of total)
Austria	3140.3	415	2.69	25.6
Belgium	3997.1	405	2.90	23.2
Denmark	2161.9	477	2.30	32.3
Finland	1938.1	385	2.44	31.6
France	24264.0	444	2.70	23.7
West Germany	27081.0	443	2.43	31.7
Greece	3700.0	260	3.19	8.5
Ireland	985.3	278	4.05	14.2
Italy	17465.5	323	2.98	13.8
Luxembourg	137.7	383	2.81	20.7
Netherlands	5384.1	372	2.59	25.5
Norway	1531.6	374	2.50	27.9
Portugal	3460.0	341	3.24	10.0
Spain	15332.9	398	2.70	10.0
Sweden	3710.0	448	2.30	32.8
Switzerland	2925.2	453	2.44	13.4
United Kingdom	22420.0	393	2.65	22.0

Source: Euromonitor, based on United Nations statistics

Of all European countries the extent of owner-occupation is largest in Greece (86 per cent), Portugal (7 per cent), Ireland (60 per cent) and Spain (58 per cent) – although in these cases it should be added that the accommodation concerned is commonly small and of a fairly modest standard. The United Kingdom, with 58 per cent home ownership, Italy (55 per cent) and France (51 per cent) are all well ahead of the bottom runners, Switzerland, Luxembourg and the Netherlands (which has only 32 per cent owner-occupation).

One-person households are most common in Sweden, where they represented 32.8 per cent of the total at the last official count. Closely following are Denmark (32.3 per cent), West Germany (31.7 per cent) and Finland (31.6 per cent), while Norway, Austria and the Netherlands are next in line with 27.9 per cent, 25.6 per cent and 25.5 per cent respectively. Single-member households are least common in Greece (8.5 per cent of the total), and in Spain and Portugal (10 per cent).

V   Standards of living

Living standards in Western Europe, while generally well above average for the developed world as a whole, have taken something of a knock from the slump of the early 1980s. Compared, for example, with the relentless rise of standards in Japan or the rapid recovery in the United States, the picture in Europe seems to have been altogether less favourable. Although West Germany, Switzerland and Luxembourg have held their own, and although Norway, the United Kingdom and Italy have made encouraging growth, it was doubtful in early 1987 whether France, Belgium, the Netherlands or Greece had managed to regain the living standards of the late 1970s.

To concentrate on material indicators of living standards: Luxembourg and West Germany have the highest per capita ownership of motor vehicles, with one car for every 2.5 persons, closely followed by Switzerland, France and Sweden with ratios of 2.6, 2.7 and 2.8 respectively. The United Kingdom has one of the lowest car ownership rates in northern Europe, at one car for every 3.4 persons – although Ireland has only one for every five inhabitants, rather less than Spain. Elsewhere in southern Europe, Greece and Portugal each run only one car for every 9.2 persons.

In 1985, around 90 per cent of all West European homes were equipped with at least one television, and about 97 per cent with a radio. Colour TVs are most common in Norway and the UK (88 per cent of all homes), Belgium (87 per cent), Sweden (86 per cent) and the Netherlands (84 per cent). In Portugal and Greece 66 per cent of all homes have a black and white set, while in Spain the proportion rises to 84 per cent.

Refrigerators and fridge freezers, a favourite measure of affluence, are found in 96 per cent of all West European homes, with the highest incidence in Austria, West Germany and Switzerland (98 per cent) and the lowest in Greece and Portugal (73 per cent and 77 per cent respectively). Washing machines are found in around 70 per cent of all homes, rising to more than 90 per cent in Italy, West Germany and the Netherlands; they are least common in Portugal (31 per cent) and in Greece (38 per cent).

Dishwashers are relatively scarce in the United Kingdom (6 per cent of all homes), in Ireland (8 per cent), in Spain (9 per cent) and in Finland (11 per cent); elsewhere in the continent (excluding Portugal and Greece, which do not supply figures), the typical ratio is around 21 per cent. Microwave ovens are a relatively new development, being largely limited in popularity to the United Kingdom (where they occupy one kitchen in five); only West Germany, Austria and Finland had made any real ground with microwaves by 1986, buying at about a fifth of the normal rate in Britain. Home video recorders, too, are almost twice as common in the UK as anywhere else, being found in one British home in three; elsewhere in Europe the typical proportion is around one in ten.

VI   Market conditions

Earlier in this chapter we looked at the development of overall European consumption, in the light of earnings and various socio-economic factors. A closer look at the pattern of spending in the various main sectors of the market reveals, however, that Europeans differ very greatly in the way they choose to spend their disposable income; this is true not only in terms of the priority which consumers ascribe to given sectors, but also of the resilience of these sectors in the face of fluctuations in the national economy.

Foodstuffs, predictably enough, represent the largest single item on the household budget for most countries – although not, incidentally, for Austria, Denmark and Sweden, all of which spend more on housing. As one would perhaps expect, the rise in food consumption, in line with increasing prosperity, tends to level off when a given stage of affluence has been reached; in 1987, Portugal, Greece and possibly Spain were still below this threshold. In many countries, especially in francophone and southern European cultures, food has a special social status which, as in the case of Belgium, is unaffected by the very high market prices. The United Kingdom is alone among EEC members in not levying value added tax on foodstuffs.

In northern Europe, food typically accounts in the mid-1980s for between 17 and 20 per cent of all consumer spending, rising in Spain and Italy to around 30 per cent, and in Portugal to a peak of 44 per cent (a good 12 percentage points higher than in 1980, incidentally). Switzerland has by far the highest per capita spending on food, at almost double the level of its nearest rival West Germany. British consumers, on the other hand, come bottom of the European league, spending only 14.3 per cent of their budgets on food in 1985, compared with 17 per cent in 1980. In most countries, although not in the UK, dairy goods are gaining favour at the expense of fish, and fresh vegetables are generally losing out to the processed foods which are gaining some acceptance even in the relatively resistant households of Greece, Italy and Spain. Meat consumption, on the whole, has been rising steadily in most countries (although, again, not in the UK).

Figures relating to the consumption of alcoholic beverages and tobacco are liable to considerable distortion because of the high proportion of duty levied by certain countries. Thus it appears that the Swiss, the Finns, the Irish and the British (who are actually among the more moderate tipplers in Europe) emerge as the biggest spenders, while the much heavier consumers in Italy, France, Austria and West Germany fare relatively well.

In general terms, European consumption of wines is undergoing a slight decline which is perhaps most noticeable in France. Beer production has been more or less stagnant for a decade, except for the lighter American-style beers which are gaining favour among younger consumers. Soft drinks are selling well all over Europe, and consumption of spirits continues to hold steady despite attempts in several Scandanavian countries to rein it in. Tobacco and tobacco products have proved surprisingly resilient since the mid-1970s in the face of public health campaigns throughout much of northern Europe; only in the United Kingdom, Austria and the Netherlands do they seem to have lost much ground in volume terms.

Sales of clothing and textiles are traditionally, and correctly, seen as a measure of the amount of spare cash in the consumer economy. They are also affected by the extent of unemployment among younger consumers, who account for at least a third of the whole market. In the mid-1980s the European clothing business has started to pull out of the serious slump which set in around 1981–1982. The upward trend has been most marked in West Germany, the second biggest per capita spender with an average outlay of $523 (1986 prices) in 1980–1985. Italy, on the other hand, is still losing out badly to foreign competition in what has become a very tight and saturated market. The United Kingdom, not normally a very vigorous market for clothes, increased its volume turnover by over 50 per cent between 1975 and 1985, accompanied by a major shake-out of retailing chains of a type which is becoming increasingly common everywhere in the continent. Footwear, while enjoying a certain stability because of the sheer need for periodic renewals, has failed to move very far from this baseline since 1980 except in Finland (where volume sales have risen by 12 per cent), the UK (up by 15 per cent) and Sweden (up by 18 per cent). Import penetration from Eastern Europe and the Far East is gaining pace even in such traditional producer nations as Portugal.

Spending on housing, heat and light accounts typically for between 21 and 25 per cent of total consumer expenditure in Europe – although, here again, differing national policies exert a drastic effect on the picture in different countries. Portugal, Greece, Ireland, Spain and the UK are notable for the high degree of owner-occupation, and the first two have until recently imposed tight controls on rents which depress the overall percentage of the budget spent on these sectors.

Subject to this qualification, we may say that Switzerland, Denmark and Sweden have by far the highest housing costs in Europe. Switzerland's per capita average of $2,584 (1980–1985) includes $2,226 for rent and only $358 for water, fuel and power, whereas Denmark's $1,818 includes $1,317 for the basic dwelling and $501 for power. Cheapest of all are Portugal and Greece, whose per capita averages of only $56 and $146 may be expected to rocket in the late 1980s as rent decontrol proceeds.

Spending on household goods and services, like clothing, tends to reflect the overall prosperity of the household as well as its feelings about the future. It has therefore been especially worrying in the early 1980s to see major durable purchases falling off quite steeply in several countries; Belgium, the Netherlands, Ireland, and especially Greece and Portugal have cut back on their household spending.

Furniture and white goods both appeared in early 1987 to be particularly badly affected. The kitchen appliances market was widely regarded as saturated, although there was still growth in microwave ovens and dishwashers, and profit margins were tight. Furniture, despite the growth of consumer credit, had only just started to pull out of the early 1980s recession which had seen volume sales in some countries decline by up to 30 per cent. Growth was strongest in West Germany and Sweden, which also represented the best of a very poor market for household textiles and soft furnishings. The United Kingdom was also doing relatively well, having raised its sales of major appliances by around 40 per cent between 1980 and 1985. There are signs of an upturn in Spain, although from a fairly low base. Household services themselves have been in steady decline throughout Europe since the mid-1980s, thanks in part to the growth of the do-it-yourself business.

West Germany and Belgium (despite the latter's problems) headed the European sales league for household goods and services with per capita averages of $804 and $824 respectively in 1980–85. France, Luxembourg and Switzerland followed with sales of between $580 and $700 each, and predictably Portugal and Greece came bottom of the table; neither appeared likely in 1987 to stage a rapid comeback.

Markets for health products and medical services tend, as one would expect, to be dominated by those countries where the state offers relatively little in the way of public health facilities. Switzerland, Belgium, France and Luxembourg are all strong purchasers of these services, spending per capita averages of $1,155, $704, $692 and $469 on the sector in 1980–1985; but West Germany ($335), the Netherlands ($866) and Austria ($296), all of which have national health services of some kind, are also contenders. Private health spending is minimal in Sweden, the United Kingdom, Greece and Portugal, where state health services predominate, but the first two have recorded reasonably strong growth since 1980 from a low starting point.

European spending on transport and communications accounts in the mid-1980s for around 17 per cent of all consumption, with Italy (almost 20 per cent) according it the highest priority; in terms of 1986 dollars, Switzerland was the biggest spender in 1980–1985, with a per capita average of $1,293; Luxembourg and West Germany (certainly the most vigorous market in 1987) followed with averages of $1,169 and $1,147 respectively. Communications are growing fastest in Italy, where per capita spending more than doubled in 1980–1985, to slightly below the European average.

TABLE 8.4 PER CAPITA CONSUMPTION OF MAJOR CONSUMPTION ITEMS
(average consumption in 1980–85; measured in December 1986 US dollars)

	Food	Alcoholic beverages	Non-alcoholic beverages	Tobacco	Textiles
Austria	1185	162	44	138	549
Belgium	1179	216	60	110	328
Denmark	1179	261	39	224	263
Finland	1135	323	a	123	257
France	1343	132	32	73	338
West Germany	1466	219	a	146	523
Greece	520	32	13	39	108
Ireland	897	395	12	153	200
Italy	1081	72	33	89	275
Luxembourg	1060	112	39	161	409
Netherlands	1034	136	56	128	406
Norway	1173	191	1	117	350
Portugal	423	21	a	19	82
Spain	813	40	a	26	211
Sweden	1185	197	102	108	363
Switzerland	2273	568	50	202	476
United Kingdom	694	335	25	157	257

a Included under the heading: Alcoholic beverages

TABLE 8.4   PER CAPITA CONSUMPTION OF MAJOR CONSUMPTION
ITEMS *continued*
(average consumption in 1980–85: measured in December 1986 US
dollars)

	Footwear	Housing	Household fuels	Household goods & services	Health
Austria	146	1099	452	466	296
Belgium	72	719	440	824	704
Denmark	55	1317	501	477	129
Finland	41	1062	b	383	144
France	84	690	375	692	692
West Germany	125	990	385	804	335
Greece	12	146	44	121	53
Ireland	44	206	203	203	123
Italy	70	388	181	281	199
Luxembourg	46	788	576	586	469
Netherlands	86	862	397	541	866
Norway	77	634	358	473	247
Portugal	20	56	b	112	42
Spain	49	370	b	222	169
Sweden	63	1550	b	397	92
Switzerland	104	2226	358	614	1155
United Kingdom	58	581	229	310	51

b Included under the heading: Housing

	Leisure & education	Transport	Communications
Austria	357	926	148
Belgium	581	765	57
Denmark	644	911	96
Finland	498	976	c
France	377	610	75
West Germany	569	1029	118
Greece	61	166	22
Ireland	314	406	23
Italy	300	512	49
Luxembourg	236	1169	c
Netherlands	646	645	86
Norway	490	819	99
Portugal	46	154	c
Spain	192	342	c
Sweden	591	855	47
Switzerland	1053	1293	c
United Kingdom	421	682	82

c Included under the heading: Transport

Source: Euromonitor, from national statistical surveys

CHAPTER NINE
FUTURE OUTLOOK

The final chapter of this handbook deals with Western Europe's economic prospects. The discussion begins by highlighting several features having an important bearing on the region's economic future. The types of issues singled out for consideration impact on growth performance, patterns of structural change, public policy and competitive abilities. As such, they are relevant both in attempting to chart the region's course of development during the next few years and in the longer term. After discussing these factors, the chapter takes a closer look at the region's short-term prospects.

I Key economic issues

Several of the issues discussed here are purely regional in scope and impact. But West Europe's economic future is also inextricably tied to events and circumstances elsewhere in the world, particularly in the USA and Japan. Thus, some of the issues considered here are truly international in character.

Among the issues which are regional in scope, the need to achieve a greater degree of market integration and economic unity has long been acknowledged but is steadily becoming increasingly important. The painfully slow progress in this field is obvious in the case of the EC but also applies within a broader context, threatening to undermine trade relations between the Community and the European Free Trade Association (EFTA). Although member countries of the EC can reflect on numerous successes, the goal of more closely integrating its respective national markets has remained elusive. The fact that many national markets are too small to support a full range of competitive industries is well known. However, structural changes within the region have created even more pressing needs. The industries which are expected to provide the growth impetus during the next ten years will require capital and R and D. These costs, coupled with comparatively brief lifetimes for many of the newer industries' products, will mean that producers must sell on a region-wide basis if they are to be competitive and profitable.

EC planners have recognized the necessity of addressing some of these problems. They have formulated Community-wide programmes to meet the high costs of R and D now being incurred in high-technology industries. Training programmes and incentives to encourage intra-European co-operation between firms have also been put together. Progress, however, has been limited. The larger member states remain reluctant to allocate more resources to the EC so long as they believe there is still a chance to go it alone. Ironically, some of the larger corporations may now be more prone to think in terms of a pan-European approach than their own governments. While they see each other less as competitors and more as potential partners, the same attitudes are less common among public authorities.

Region-wide progress towards greater market integration is also threatened by fundamental differences in the approaches of the EC and EFTA. The EC is a supranational organization with political as well as economic ambitions. In contrast, EFTA remains a coalition of small countries concerned only with free trade. Exporters in EFTA countries are heavily dependent on EC markets. The group is also the Community's biggest trading partner, surpassing even the USA and Japan. But as the Community slowly proceeds towards its goal of a completely free internal market, there is a growing danger that EC–EFTA trade will suffer. EFTA's free-trade accords with the EC apply only to industrial goods and not to agriculture or services. And while there are no tariffs on trade in manufactures, the EC imposes stringent requirements on 'product origin'. It will not extend free trade treatment unless a large proportion of the exported product originates in the EFTA country.[1] Because of the small size of domestic markets in all EFTA countries, the lowest-cost suppliers of many components and materials are usually

---

[1] This requirement is supplemented by an array of technical barriers regarding EC specifications on product size, composition and safety.

144

foreign. Unless EFTA succeeds in drawing closer to the EC, the natural trend toward increasing product specialization can run foul of existing rules on product origin and constitute a significant barrier to intra-European trade.

A second regional issue of crucial importance is the persistence and severity of the unemployment problem. Most conventional interpretations attribute much of the rise in unemployment to the stringent monetary and fiscal policies adopted by governments in order to control inflation. The continuation of such policies over a comparatively long period probably contributed to the slump in output and the dramatic rise of unemployment. However, the presumed relationship between inflation and unemployment now appears to be more complex than was previously thought. Traditional analysis assumed that a stable rate of inflation would be consistent with a particular rate of unemployment, known to economists by the cumbersome title of the non-accelerating-inflation rate of unemployment (NAIRU). In periods when unemployment exceeds the NAIRU, wage demands would moderate and the pace of inflation should abate. Conversely, when unemployment is less than the NAIRU benchmark, increasing wage pressure would lead to accelerating inflation.

Economists expected minor variations in the NAIRU over time but the experience of Western Europe has now led many to believe that they have overlooked an important feature – the possibility that a persistently high rate of unemployment may eventually raise the NAIRU as well. The result is a large pool of unemployed whose existence has no impact on wage behaviour. This interpretation suggests that a 'discourage worker' effect (i.e. the eventual withdrawal of persons from the labour force because they cannot find a job) now appears to operate in much of West Europe. The longer a person is out of a job, the less able/willing he is to compete. And because an increasing proportion of the labour force is among the long-term unemployed, there is less competition for jobs and therefore a rising NAIRU.

The new line of reasoning has implications for government policy regarding inflation as well as employment. If the NAIRU accounts for a larger portion of total unemployment than was thought, policies designed to boost demand would have a higher inflationary risk than previously believed. Similarly, if unemployment can be raised more easily than it is reduced, the costs of cutting inflation are higher than government officials had thought. These facts point to the need to take supply-side measures to reduce the NAIRU. Examples might include lower payroll taxes and reduced income taxes for those in poorly paying jobs. And if long-term unemployment is a powerful force driving the NAIRU upward, job schemes will have to be focused increasingly on those out of work for more than six months. In summary, the continuing burden of unemployment will force West European governments to begin experimenting with supply-side approaches to their common problem.

The unemployment problem, however, cannot be considered in isolation from the need to develop the labour skills appropriate for tomorrow's industries. Success in this regard will have more than regional implications: West Europe's future standing in the industrialized world will also depend on the outcome. Governments, businesses or a combination of the two will have to pay for such programmes and the cost will be massive. The growing attention devoted to this issue is partly the result of a fundamental change in the way industrialized countries function. Though technology has always exerted considerable influence on the way economies work, its relations with other economic inputs – notably labour – has begun to change in unforeseen ways. More than ever before, the key ingredient for creating new wealth is not land, labour, capital or other physical inputs but, rather, technological know-how.

This shift in factor significance is underlined by European studies showing that in other industrialized countries only 15 per cent of total productivity growth is accounted for by labour. Another 25 per cent of all productivity growth was attributed to capital investment while at least 60 per cent was the result of technological change. The implications of these estimates are twofold. One is that in order to remain competitive with its international rivals, West Europe will have to take serious steps to upgrade the quality of its workforce. A second implication of the closer relationship between productivity growth and technological know-how concerns West Europe's need to develop more of its own technologies. For today's workers, a prime difficulty associated with the accelerating pace of technological innovation is the growing obsolesence of their technical abilities. The effective life span of a worker's knowledge is now shrinking so rapidly that it is not much longer than the time needed to acquire that knowledge. Engineers or computer scientists who completed their education in 1987 will find that at least half the knowledge they have accumulated will become irrelevant by 1992. These individuals will soon have to return to university for further training if their firms are serious about keeping abreast of competitors. The trend can be even more wrenching for those whose educational background is modest. Occupational adjustments that could once be made over generations – for example, the tractor, telegraph or typewriter – must now be accepted instantly. Furthermore, the frequency of today's occupational changes is high, sometimes occurring three or four times within a working career. The consequence of all these changes is that many of the skills necessary for West Europe's continued technological progress are either missing or are in extremely short supply.

At the forefront in the explosion of knowledge are advances in computers, databases, decision-making software, CAD terminals, bits of office automation equipment and other devices all lumped together as 'information technologies'. These new technologies have already reduced the number of jobs in manufacturing and are now beginning to do the same in services. New jobs can, of course, be created. But the new technologies which eliminate jobs are not necessarily the same as those which create them. Countries benefiting from new job creation will be those which have efficient work forces, in particular countries with workers who are literate in the new information technologies. Given the labour rigidities in West Europe, most countries would seem to have little choice but to allow their service sectors to grow unhampered while channelling a growing portion of their support into training. Training for unspecified jobs is a risky process, particularly when technologies are changing as rapidly as today. Nevertheless, a shortage of European skills in vital areas such as software programming and CAD is already becoming apparent. A much larger investment in training will be needed if the region is to avoid the technological illiteracies which will aggravate its employment problem and act as a drag on economic growth.

In the longer run the region will have to hasten the development of its own new technologies if it hopes to maintain a base of economic wealth which is comparable to that of North America or Japan. The region's economies have grown only feebly throughout the present upswing while their ability to provide new jobs has been weaker still. When this performance is compared with the American or Japanese economies, many conclude that the European ability to compete is being eroded. Pessimists frequently point to the Europeans' apparent inability to stay abreast of their rivals in high-technology industries.

The implication that West Europe is on the wrong side of a technology gap can be questioned. Today's concepts of high technology provide no more than a vague benchmark for judging international standards of performance. Moreover, even according to the most meticulous of definitions, the region can count a number of successes. European firms can claim to be on the technological frontiers in several industries, among them nuclear power, aircraft and aerospace. The list of successes is even longer when the specialities of individual countries are taken into account. In the latter sense, specific West European countries are among the world's leaders in pharmaceuticals, telecommunications, military technology, computer software and other fields.

Despite these successes, West Europeans have reason to be concerned about the pace of technological change in their region. One is the region's comparatively poor performance in crucial parts of the electronics industry such as the production of hardware and the software used to process information. The most disturbing feature of this equation is the slow pace at which the new technologies emanating from the industry are being absorbed by European firms. For example, West Europe's share of world consumption of semiconductor chips has fallen significantly in the period since 1972. The region's waning technological standing is further suggested by a similar downward trend in its share of world production of these components.

Europe's ability to absorb technological advances in electronics by purchasing them from abroad is also being undermined at a time when its ability to produce new products is lagging. West Europe buys much of its technology from Japan or the USA to be incorporated into its own products and processes. The growing sophistication of these products means that long periods are required between conception and sales. The immense investments needed for this purpose must then be recouped within 2–4 years. These circumstances have at least three undesirable implications for those who would rely heavily on foreign suppliers. First, some of the developers of new technologies have become more reluctant to license them to others. Second, the growing complexities of the latest technologies make it difficult for the purchaser to master them in time to market products which have a steadily shortening lifetime. Finally, inter-firm collaboration between the producers and users of new technologies has become common practice in many fields including computers, telecommunications, semiconductors, industrial robots, etc. But the trend towards closer co-operation favours firms which work in close proximity or share the same geographical markets. That attribute is true of American and Japanese firms producing microprocessors, automated machinery and other components. In contrast, the sparsity of such inter-firm contacts in West Europe means that they often master the basic workings of their next-generation machines far later than their competitors.

Europe's technological weakness should also be seen in terms of its industrial structure. The economic turbulence and disruption created by the emergence of new technologies has yet to affect Europe in the same way as Japan or the USA. In the latter markets large numbers of new companies have been created which, in turn, have spawned a host of new ideas. Most of the new entrants have quickly died, though the survivors have often grown into big firms. In the process, many of the long-established American and Japanese firms have been forced to adapt, recognizing that they could not survive if they strive for stability.

The pace of entry and exit in high-technology industries appears to be much more leisurely in Europe than in the USA or Japan. A corollary is that the degree of stability in Europe's industries is greater than that of its major international rivals. Seen in this context, Europe's problem is that it values stability at a time when this feature represents a comparative disadvantage. The limited evidence available, not only for Europe but also for Japan and the USA, shows that the bulk of new employment opportunities is created by firms which are smaller and younger than the industry average.Thus the preference for stability can be a dangerous one in the sense that each new high-tech job results in the creation of a multiple number of low-tech jobs.

In conclusion, none of the problems mentioned here can really be seen in isolation. The limitations of small domestic markets, the mounting costs of unemployment and the painfully slow pace of technological progress and adjustment not only act as a significant drag on Europe's growth but are also inter-related to some extent. Governments and firms alike will have to devote more of their energies and resources to these issues than they have done in the past. To the extent that these efforts are successful, the region's economic prospects which are sketched in the following section will be considerably improved.

II Economic outlook

Most of the forecasts drawn up at the end of 1986 pointed to a continuation in the modest pace of growth (approximately 2.5 per cent) which had prevailed during the two previous years. However, growth of output in the second half of 1986 was flat and that trend continued into 1987. With such a discouraging performance, the number of optimists has dwindled. Short-term growth prospects have been gradually reduced. The overall impression is that the economic upswing of the past four years has begun to show clear signs of weakness. Current forecasts of growth in output in West Europe indicate a range of 2.2 to 2.5 per cent in 1987.

The EC, too, has scaled back its short-term forecasts for growth. In late 1986, the Community predicted a growth rate for real GDP of 2.8 per cent in the next year. A much less optimistic set of projections was published in mid-1987. The EC's executive body has now cut back its forecast for growth of GDP to 2.2 per cent in 1987. The new figure implies a slowdown in the rate of expansion in comparison with 1986 when real GDP grew by 2.5 per cent (see Table 4.1). Only a slight improvement is now expected in 1988 when GDP is forecast to grow by 2.3 per cent.

Table 9.1 shows country forecasts made in mid-1987. The major reason for the Community's reduced expectations is the slowdown which is forecast for West Germany. After growing at 2.5 per cent in 1986, the German GDP was projected to rise by only 1.5 per cent in 1987 and 2 per cent in 1988. Because West Germany buys roughly one-quarter of its Community partners' exports, a slowdown in that country will impair growth throughout the region. Most of the smaller countries in the EC are expected to grow very slowly. Belgium and the Netherlands are heavily dependent on the German market through their trade links. Real GDP in those two countries is likely to grow by little more than 1.5 per cent and is expected to fall in Denmark and Greece.

TABLE 9.1   GDP^a FORECASTS, SELECTED EUROPEAN COUNTRIES
(annual percentage change)

	1987	1988
Belgium	1.2	2.1
Denmark	−0.2	0.5
France	1.5	1.8
Greece	−0.7	0.9
Ireland	1.1	1.6
Italy	3.2	2.8
Netherlands	1.7	1.1
Portugal	3.4	3.0
Spain	2.8	3.0
United Kingdom	3.1	2.6
West Germany	1.5	2.0

Source: OECD
^{a} real output

Economic growth in the United Kingdom should be one of the highest rates in the EC, 3.1 per cent in 1987 and 2.6 per cent in 1988. The acceleration should lead to a fall in British unemployment, from 12 per cent in 1986 to 11.3 per cent in 1987 and 10.8 per cent in 1988. Similar improvements are not expected on a Community-wide basis – unemployment is expected to stabilize at 11.8 per cent.

Whatever the forecast, there is widespread agreement that most countries will have to continue to rely upon domestic demands as the major source of growth. Public authorities, in turn, will continue to put their hopes on private consumption as the main source for demand expansion. But as the effects of the gains in real income resulting from past improvements in the terms of trade wear off, the prospects for growth in private consumption are likely to weaken. Alternatively, the growth of domestic demand will have to be bolstered through policy measures such as tax cuts or increased government spending. These moves, however, would be counter to the generally tight fiscal approaches embraced by most West European governments.

The deceleration in growth of private consumption may be especially pronounced in some of the smaller economies, notably Belgium, Denmark and Norway. The outlook is somewhat better for Spain and Portugal, owing in part to those countries' recent entry to the EC. Growth of domestic demand will likely slacken in Spain during 1987–8 but should be offset by a smaller negative balance of trade. Similar expectations apply to Portugal where a general easing in macroeconomic policies will be continued, thus providing an additional stimulus to domestic demand. A different situation will prevail in Greece. Policies in that country are likely to become more restrictive over the next few years and lead to some slowdown in growth of domestic demand.

Among the larger countries, the economic outlook in West Germany will be crucial to the region's performance during the remainder of this decade. The country recorded virtually no growth in the second half of 1986 and indicators for early 1987 showed a continuation of that trend. Accordingly, West German economists have steadily scaled down their hopes. Current forecasts by German institutes now suggest that without new growth-stimulating policies, GNP may have expanded by only 1–2 per cent in 1987. As growth has slowed, domestic pressure has been added to American insistence that the government use tax cuts to stimulate demand. Those cuts scheduled for 1988 have already been increased but many senior officials are now privately advocating that the 1990 package of DM44 billion be moved forward. Others have proposed that the government use the provisions of the stability and growth law which allows it to make tax cuts across the board without new legislation. The stimulation of domestic demand is the focus of all these pleas.

A major reason for the increasingly pessimistic forecasts for overall growth in West Germany is the unfavourable outlook for exports and the depressing effects of the real trade balance. Although the global economy is expected to grow by 2–3 per cent in the short term, West Germany is not well-positioned to benefit. Most of its exports are capital goods, while the expected expansion is seen as coming from higher demand for services and consumer goods. Conversely, the export prospects of Italy, France and the United Kingdom appear to have improved slightly since the beginning of 1987. The change in outlook is due not only to stronger demand in West Germany but is also a result of gains in competitiveness due to exchange rate shifts. These hopes are contingent, however, on a rate of growth in West German demand which would not be significantly less than recent levels. A much reduced rate of growth would have repercussions for export prospects throughout the region – especially since export demand in non-European markets is likely to remain depressed for the foreseeable future.

The relative optimism which characterized many of the forecasts made in 1986 was partly based on the expectation that the fall in oil prices would provide a much needed boost to growth. The presumption was that the negative effects of previous increases in the price of oil would now be reversed. However, previous oil shocks not only led to a fall in real income but also resulted in an output loss as capital stock was adjusted to a new set of relative prices. The 1986 drop in oil prices may compensate for earlier losses in real income but it, too, will have a 'structural loss of output' all its own. Subsequent adjustments in output will be required in order to accommodate the latest shift in relative factor prices and will mean further increases in investment.

Official forecasts for the growth of total real fixed investment are not promising, however. Among the four largest West European countries, investment is expected to move upward strongly in Italy, though it will increase only moderately in France and the United Kingdom and appears unlikely to change in West Germany. Changes in the composition will include a deceleration of investment in machinery and equipment. In several of the larger countries, this slowdown should be offset by higher growth rates for investment in structures and buildings. Growth of total investment, however, is expected to slacken in most of the smaller West European countries.

Any deterioration in the competitiveness of the external sector in major European economies (and especially in West Germany) will have an additional negative impact on growth of fixed investment. Relative to the 1960s and early 1970s, West Europe has already experienced a substantial deceleration in investment. A further cutback would have at least two serious complications. First, the share of gross investment serving to offset the scrapping of old equipment is already large and a further slowdown can only increase this proportion. Second, deceleration of gross investment implies a slowdown in the rate at which technological advances become available and are introduced into the production process. The pace of technological advancement has already been singled out in the first section of this chapter, and such a trend could only worsen the region's current standing in this field. To avoid such an outcome, more expansionary fiscal policies would be needed so as to encourage a higher level of fixed investment. These moves, however, would require a degree of pan-European co-ordination which, heretofore, has not been realized.

With regard to the current account and balance of trade, West Europe's gap between growth of imports and that of exports should decline in the coming months. Official national forecasts assembled in late 1986 anticipated an increase in growth of exports of 2 to 4 per cent in 1987 coupled with a decline in the import growth rate of 5 to 6 per cent. Corresponding OECD forecasts put export growth at 2.5 per cent while imports were projected to expand at 4.75 per cent. These figures are, of course, predicated on a set of exchange rate adjustments which are, themselves, extremely difficult to forecast. Trends in early 1987 suggest that export performance may be only slightly depressed by the substantial fall in the dollar during the first quarter of this year. On the other hand, West Europe's imports from Asia – and mainly from Japan – have begun to rise rapidly as that region's exporters shift their sights from the USA to West Europe.

Most countries benefited considerably from terms-of-trade gains in 1986. In the absence of such gains, trade balances would have deteriorated substantially as the volume of exports rose much more slowly than that of imports. The above forecasts would imply some narrowing in the gap between the two sets of growth rates in the future. Among the larger countries, a rise in exports to non-oil developing countries should be one contributory feature. This trend is likely to be partially offset by a continued decline in exports to oil-producing developing countries.

The outlook for trade balances in some of the smaller West European countries is somewhat different. In Spain expectations are for some improvement in export performance coupled with a slight slowdown in the growth of imports. Altogether, Spain's current account surplus should have increased in 1987. Prospects for the balance of trade in Portugal are somewhat more precarious. A reduction in the current account surplus is forecast on the basis of no further change in the country's terms of trade and a small decline in net transfers. Greece can look forward to a rise in earnings from tourism. This development, coupled with a gain in net exports, should lead to a smaller current account deficit in that country.

In national currency terms no dramatic changes in the prices of traded goods are foreseen in the near future. In 1986, prices of manufactures fell in national currencies as exporters in countries with appreciating currencies reduced their profit margins. No similar trend is likely to have emerged in 1987–8. The region's trade balance now appears likely to deteriorate in national currency terms as the growth in trade volume will not be offset by terms of trade gains.

Prospects are more promising in the case of inflation. The outlook for Western Europe is subject to some uncertainty, owing in part to future movements in exchange rates and oil prices. With this qualification, consumer prices are expected to rise at rates of 2.5 to 3.0 per cent during 1987–8 – only slightly higher than the current pace. In most countries the underlying rate of domestic cost inflation should remain low. Wage pressures should continue to be relatively moderate and further declines in interest rates could occur in some countries. The absence of any severe inflationary threat should allow public authorities somewhat greater flexibility in the future to deal with the unemployment problem – for example, to introduce some of the supply-side measures noted in the first section of this chapter.

Inflationary prospects are not equally bright for all West European countries. The outlook for inflation is much more tentative in some countries, for example, in Spain, Portugal and Greece. In Spain, the expected decline is intended to be a sharp one but the government has achieved only moderate success in controlling prices in recent years. More restrictive policies in Greece should lead to a continuing fall in inflation although the government's target of 10 per cent in 1987 is not likely to be realized. A similar downward trend should occur in Portugal but here, too, the expectations for a significant decline in inflation may prove to be overly optimistic. Favourable external factors made an important contribution to inflation control in 1986 and similar effects are unlikely to be repeated in the short term.

Future trends in patterns of consumption, investment and trade will have important repercussions for labour market conditions in West Europe. Because the issues of employment and unemployment are now seen in a political and social context as well as an economic one, the pressure to react to these problems will escalate. Two factors, the population size of working age and the participation rate, are of fundamental importance for the supply of labour. With regard to the first of these factors, the decline in fertility rates which began in the late 1960s has now begun to affect the growth of West Europe's population of working age. The effects of this demographic change will require another fifteen years before they are fully reflected in the total working age population. Nevertheless, during that period the growth of one segment of the total working age population, the central age group (25–54 years), will slow down substantially. For the region as a whole, this structural shift should lead to a substantial easing of labour market pressures.

The only exceptions to the downward trend in the size of the central age group will be Ireland and France. Because unemployment prospects in France are especially discouraging, they deserve special mention. Unlike Italy, the United Kingdom or West Germany, the number of unemployed French workers is expected to rise markedly. In line with present trends, the number of jobs will continue to fall while the labour force should grow until the mid-1990s. Pressures to accept early retirement and a rise in the entry age of new workers owing to additional education and training will help to ameliorate the situation but will be insufficient to reverse the overall trend. Similarly, public investment programmes which will create new jobs will have little effect for several years. Altogether, between 1987 and 1992, the forecast is for an additional one million unemployed.

Changes in the age structure of the population will be another feature helping to reduce the growth of the labour force. Based on the assumption of unchanged activity rates, the growth of Western Europe's work force should be reduced to nil by the end of this century, equivalent to a decline in the current growth rate of roughly 40 per cent. However, the prognosis is less promising for the short-term. The labour force will continue to grow more rapidly than the population of the working age, until the early 1990s. Prior to that time, any reduction in demographic pressure on the labour market will be due to the shrinking number of young workers (15–24 years) and workers over 55.

Variations in rates of worker participation will blur the relationship between changes in the labour force and in the working age population. In recent years the most important variable governing the participation rate has been the growing feminization of the work force. In some countries – notably Belgium, Sweden, Switzerland and West Germany – the absolute number of males in the work force has begun to decline but has been more than offset by increases in the number of working women. The female labour force tends to grow much more rapidly that the male labour force during recessions. Because of this characteristic and in view of the overall outlook for growth in the new few years, changes in participation rates can be expected to aggravate the unemployment situation in Western Europe. More generally, the overall expectation is that short-run changes in employment/unemployment trends will result in little improvement. Increases in levels of employment are likely to be very small during the next two years while unemployment rates, at best, will remain unchanged.

In conclusion, the region's short-term outlook is a mixed one. On the darker side, the problems faced by West European economies are by no means transient or cyclical in nature. Unemployment, market fragmentation, a perenially sluggish rate of investment and the comparatively slow pace of technological development and its application will all have consequences extending well into the 1990s. At the global level, the pace of structural and technological change prevailing today is not compatible with the staid and cautious approaches which are so common in West Europe. Problems such as those discussed here will be difficult to address and are not amenable to short-term solutions. On the other hand, the region retains many advantages. It is rich in human and capital resources and its 350 million consumers represent a potential market which would surpass that of any other industrialized area. Nor will West Europe's position in the world economy be undermined by any lack of materials or markets. But in a world which is now in the midst of deep technological and economic change an approach based on natural caution is questionable and risks a worsening of the region's most serious problems.

FACT FILE ONE

TABLE A. PRIVATE CONSUMPTION DEFLATORS
(percentage change from previous period)

	1985	1986	1987	1988[a]
Austria	3.4	1.5	2.0	2.1
Belgium	5.0	1.2	1.2	—
Denmark	4.7	3.5	4.0	4.3
Finland	6.0	3.3	3.0	—
France	5.5	2.2	2.0	2.0
Greece	18.6	22.3	15.5	15.0
Ireland	4.2	4.0	3.5	—
Italy	9.4	6.3	4.0	3.8
Netherlands	2.6	0.0	−0.5	—
Norway	5.8	7.3	8.2	—
Portugal	19.8	12.0	10.5	—
Spain	8.8	8.5	6.4	—
Sweden	7.2	4.5	3.8	—
Switzerland	3.6	0.8	1.3	1.1
United Kingdom	5.2	4.0	4.5	4.8
West Germany	2.2	−0.8	1.0	1.5

Source: OECD and author's estimates
[a] Forecasts are for the first half of 1988

TABLE B. RECENT AND EXPECTED TRENDS IN EMPLOYMENT AND UNEMPLOYMENT
(percentage change over previous year)

	Employment			Unemployment			
	1985	1986	1987	1985	1986	1987	1988
Austria	0.0	0.2	0.2	3.6	4.0	4.3	—
Belgium	0.3	0.2	−0.3	12.1	11.8	11.3	12.0
Denmark	2.4	2.7	0.5	8.9	7.8	8.5	—
Finland	1.0	0.0	−0.3	6.3	9.3	10.0	—
France	−0.1	0.0	−0.5	10.2	10.5	11.4	12.0
Greece	0.5	0.0	−0.3	8.4	9.2	10.2	—
Ireland	−3.2	−1.0	0.0	17.3	18.0	18.0	—
Italy	0.5	0.3	0.5	10.6	11.3	11.5	11.7
Netherlands	1.1	1.0	0.7	14.3	13.5	13.0	12.8
Norway	2.1	2.7	1.0	2.5	2.0	2.5	—
Portugal	−0.5	0.5	0.5	10.2	10.0	9.8	—
Spain	−0.9	1.8	1.5	21.9	21.5	21.2	20.5
Sweden	1.0	0.7	0.2	2.8	2.5	2.8	2.5
Switzerland	0.9	1.0	0.8	1.0	1.0	1.0	1.0
United Kingdom	1.3	0.8	1.0	11.8	11.7	11.5	10.8
West Germany	0.7	0.0	0.7	8.3	7.8	7.5	8.3

Source: OECD, ECE, national forecasts and author's estimates

REAL PRIVATE CONSUMPTION
Percentage change over preceding year

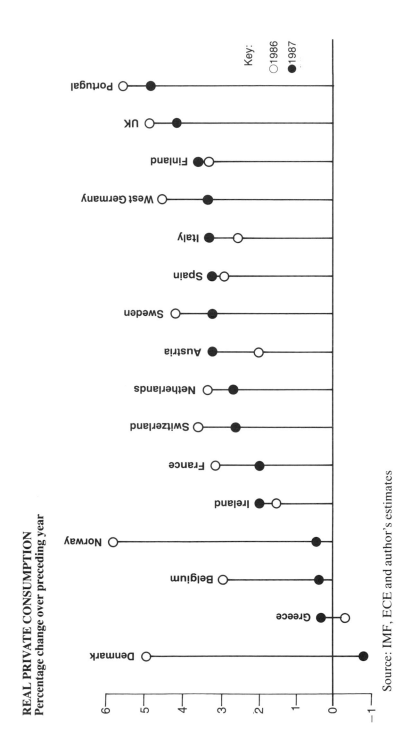

Key: ○1986 ●1987

Source: IMF, ECE and author's estimates

TABLE C.   **WEST GERMANY'S ECONOMIC PERFORMANCE
AND RECENT FORECASTS**
(percentage change over previous year)

	1985	1986	1987
GNP	2.5	2.5	1.5
Consumer prices	2.2	−0.2	0.0 to 1.0
Private consumption	1.8	4.1	3.0 to 4.0
Government consumption	2.2	2.5	2.0 to 3.0
Gross fixed investment	−0.3	3.1	3.5
Domestic demand	1.5	3.8	3.5 to 4.0
Exports	7.3	−0.6	−0.5
Imports	4.7	3.1	3.5
Number employed	0.7	1.0	0.5 to 1.0

Source: National forecasts by independent research institutes and official government projections

FACT FILE TWO

TABLE 1.   GROSS DOMESTIC PRODUCT, AT CURRENT PRICES

	Unit	1980	1981	1982	1983	1984	1985
Austria	Bn Sch	994.7	1056.0	1133.5	1202.0	1285.2	1366.6
Belgium	Bn BFr	3519.0	3646.0	3972.0	4209.0	4511.0	4812.0
Cyprus	M C£	754.5	870.6	1015.5	1124.1	1315.7	1360.0
Denmark	Bn Kr	373.8	407.8	464.5	513.2	561.1	605.3
Finland	Bn Ma	192.6	218.5	245.2	274.4	307.9	334.9
France	Bn Fr	2769.3	3110.6	3567.0	3935.0	4283.0	4597.2
West Germany	Bn DM	1478.9	1540.9	1597.9	1674.8	1754.3	1839.9
Greece	Bn Dr	1711.0	2046.8	2552.3	3052.0	3769.8	4527.1
Ireland	M I£	9361.0	11359.0	13326.0	14451.0	16106.0	17254.0
Italy	'000Bn L	338.7	401.6	470.5	538.9	615.1	684.8
Luxembourg	Bn LFr	147.7	158.1	181.0	207.8	227.5	247.0
Netherlands	Bn G	336.7	352.9	368.9	381.0	394.9	412.5
Norway	Bn Kr	285.1	327.7	362.3	402.2	452.7	497.8
Portugal	Bn Esc	1231.5	1465.4	1848.0	2279.2	2805.5	3524.8
Spain	Bn Pts	15185.0	17327.0	19870.0	22778.0	25935.0	29000.0
Sweden	Bn Kr	525.1	573.0	627.7	705.4	789.6	862.5
Switzerland	Bn SFr	170.3	184.8	196.0	203.9	214.1	227.8
Turkey	Bn TL	4328.0	6413.6	8578.0	11467.8	18188.0	27000.0
United Kingdom	Bn £	230.0	253.9	276.2	301.1	320.2	351.6

Source: IMF

TABLE 2.   GROSS DOMESTIC PRODUCT, IN BILLIONS OF CURRENT US DOLLARS

	1980	1981	1982	1983	1984	1985
Austria	72.0	66.5	67.9	62.1	58.3	79.1
Belgium	111.6	94.8	84.7	75.7	71.5	95.6
Cyprus	0.3	0.4	0.5	0.6	0.8	0.7
Denmark	62.1	55.7	55.4	52.0	49.8	69.6
Finland	50.2	50.1	42.2	47.2	47.2	61.8
France	613.2	541.2	530.4	471.4	446.5	608.0
West Germany	754.9	683.4	672.4	614.9	557.3	747.5
Greece	36.8	35.5	38.2	30.9	29.3	30.6
Ireland	17.8	17.9	18.6	16.4	16.0	19.0
Italy	364.0	334.7	343.4	324.7	317.7	407.9
Luxembourg	3.7	4.1	3.9	3.7	3.6	4.9
Netherlands	158.1	143.0	140.6	128.9	111.3	148.8
Norway	55.0	56.4	51.4	55.7	49.8	68.5
Portugal	23.2	22.5	20.8	17.3	16.7	22.4
Spain	191.6	177.8	158.2	145.4	149.6	188.1
Sweden	120.1	102.9	86.1	88.2	87.8	113.3
Switzerland	96.6	102.8	98.3	93.6	82.2	109.7
Turkey	48.0	48.0	·45.9	40.6	40.9	46.8
United Kingdom	549.3	502.9	446.2	436.8	370.3	455.8

Source: Euromonitor

TABLE 3. PER CAPITA GROSS DOMESTIC PRODUCT, 1980 AND 1985, IN CURRENT AND 1986 US DOLLARS

| | 1980 | | 1985 | |
	Current	Dec. 1986	Current	Dec. 1986
Austria	9540	9597	10461	13185
Belgium	11333	8840	9681	12065
Cyprus	3283	2340	3736	3967
Denmark	12138	9994	13181	16100
Finland	10493	8405	12643	14286
France	11381	7962	11020	12908
West Germany	12263	12377	12190	15460
Greece	3813	1279	3098	3299
Ireland	5225	3853	6044	6802
Italy	6450	4420	7141	8827
Luxembourg	13015	10153	13624	16978
Netherlands	11182	10863	10277	12996
Norway	13457	9420	15820	16210
Portugal	2350	853	2358	2459
Spain	5104	3055	4874	5674
Sweden	14450	9806	13547	15130
Switzerland	15112	16416	17297	22027
Turkey	1080	129	950	723
United Kingdom	9817	6069	9050	9238

Source: Euromonitor

TABLE 4. DEVELOPMENT OF REAL GROSS DOMESTIC PRODUCT (base: 1980 = 100)

	1980	1981	1982	1983	1984	1985	1986e
Austria	100.0	99.8	101.0	103.0	105.1	108.2	110.0
Belgium	100.0	98.5	99.9	99.7	101.6	102.9	105.3
Cyprus	100.0	103.0	108.0	110.7	119.1	n.a.	n.a.
Denmark	100.0	99.1	102.1	104.3	107.9	110.8	114.6
Finland	100.0	101.9	104.8	107.9	111.1	114.0	116.1
France	100.0	100.5	102.3	103.0	104.6	106.1	108.2
West Germany	100.0	100.0	99.0	100.8	103.9	106.4	103.2
Greece	100.0	100.5	102.3	103.0	104.6	106.1	107.5
Ireland	100.0	103.3	104.8	102.8	107.1	109.2	108.7
Italy	100.0	100.2	99.7	99.2	101.8	104.1	107.0
Luxembourg	100.0	100.6	101.3	93.4	88.9	91.5	93.2
Netherlands	100.0	99.3	97.8	99.5	101.6	103.6	105.6
Norway	100.0	100.9	101.2	105.8	111.7	116.4	120.8
Portugal	100.0	105.1	109.1	103.0	101.4	104.7	109.7
Spain	100.0	100.3	101.3	103.8	106.2	108.5	111.8
Sweden	100.0	99.7	100.5	102.9	107.0	109.4	110.8
Switzerland	100.0	101.5	100.4	101.0	103.0	98.8	102.6
Turkey	100.0	104.1	108.8	112.5	119.1	125.2	135.2
United Kingdom	100.0	98.8	99.8	103.6	105.8	109.7	112.4

Source: Euromonitor/International Monetary Fund/Organization for Economic Co-operation and Development (OECD)

TABLE 5. COMPOSITION OF GROSS DOMESTIC PRODUCT
Figures for 1985, except where denoted otherwise
(%)

	Agriculture	Manufacturing	Construction	Services
Austria	3.8	34.8	7.6	53.8
Belgium (1984)	2.5	24.7	5.4	67.4
Cyprus (1983)	9.7	18.6	12.5	59.2
Denmark	5.8	23.5	6.0	64.8
Finland	8.4	29.9	8.0	53.7
France (1984)	4.3	31.7	6.2	57.8
West Germany	1.7	36.7	5.1	56.5
Greece	17.4	17.9	6.6	58.1
Ireland (1984)	12.3	35.6	7.0	45.1
Italy	6.7	34.7	5.7	52.9
Luxembourg	n.a	n.a	n.a	n.a
Netherlands	4.1	28.7	5.6	61.6
Norway	3.6	32.3	5.2	58.9
Portugal (1984)	9.2	31.8	6.2	52.8
Spain	6.4	28.6	6.7	58.3
Sweden	3.3	24.9	7.2	64.8
Switzerland	1.8	26.0	14.0	58.2
Turkey	21.8	24.4	5.8	48.0
United Kingdom	2.1	24.4	5.7	67.8

Source: National statistics/IMF/Euromonitor

TABLE 6. GROSS DOMESTIC PRODUCT ACCORDING TO
DEMAND STRUCTURE, 1985
(%)

	Private consumption	Government consumption	Fixed investment	Exports	Imports	Stock-building
Austria	56.5	18.5	22.1	40.0	−39.7	2.6
Belgium	65.0	17.9	15.5	74.5	−72.8	−0.2
Cyprus (1983)	64.5	17.3	29.2	53.4	−66.4	1.8
Denmark	54.1	25.3	19.2	37.5	−37.0	0.9
Finland	54.1	19.7	24.0	29.5	−28.2	0.9
France	65.0	16.5	18.8	23.5	−24.0	0.1
West Germany	55.9	20.0	20.4	34.3	−31.5	0.9
Greece	65.5	19.9	10.0	21.6	−33.4	1.6
Ireland	57.5	18.6	20.8	61.2	−58.5	0.4
Italy	63.4	20.0	18.2	25.4	−27.8	0.7
Luxembourg (1984)	57.9	15.7	22.2	97.0	−96.0	3.2
Netherlands	58.9	16.3	18.4	64.5	−58.9	0.8
Norway	48.6	18.6	21.7	47.2	−39.3	3.2
Portugal	67.1	14.7	21.3	39.8	−42.8	−0.2
Spain	66.4	12.3	18.5	22.5	−19.9	0.2
Sweden	50.9	27.7	19.0	35.3	−32.8	−0.1
Switzerland (1986)	60.3	13.2	23.8	37.4	−35.7	1.0
Turkey	72.9	10.1	32.4	18.9	−22.5	1.6
United Kingdom	60.4	21.1	17.1	29.6	−28.4	0.2

Source: IMF/Euromonitor

TABLE 7.   THE ROLE OF GOVERNMENT SPENDING IN THE ECONOMY
Total government spending (including investment) as a percentage of
gross domestic product

	1970	1980	1982	1983	1984	1985
Austria	39.2	48.9	50.9	51.4	50.8	50.7
Belgium	36.5	50.8	55.7	55.6	55.0	54.4
Cyprus	n.a.	n.a.	n.a.	n.a.	n.a.	n.a.
Denmark	40.2	56.2	61.2	61.6	60.9	59.5
Finland	30.5	36.5	39.0	40.3	39.9	41.5
France	38.9	46.4	51.1	52.0	52.7	52.4
West Germany	38.6	48.3	49.4	48.3	48.0	47.2
Greece	22.4	30.5	37.3	38.5	40.2	43.2
Ireland	39.6	50.9	55.6	56.3	54.6	n.a.
Italy	34.2	46.1	54.8	57.0	57.4	58.4
Luxembourg	33.1	54.8	56.4	n.a.	n.a.	n.a.
Netherlands	43.9	57.5	61.6	62.2	61.3	60.2
Norway	41.0	50.7	50.8	50.9	48.5	48.1
Portugal	21.6	25.9	43.9	n.a.	n.a.	n.a.
Spain	22.2	32.9	37.5	38.8	39.3	n.a.
Sweden	43.3	61.6	66.6	66.2	63.5	64.5
Switzerland	21.3	29.3	30.1	30.9	31.4	30.9
Turkey	21.9	n.a.	n.a.	n.a.	n.a.	n.a.
United Kingdom	39.8	45.1	47.4	47.2	47.8	n.a.

Source: Organization for Economic Co-operation and Development (OECD)

TABLE 8.   EXPORTS (FOB), IN MILLIONS OF CURRENT US DOLLARS

	1980	1981	1982	1983	1984	1985	1986
Austria	17027	15603	15363	15155	15329	16955	21835
Belgium/Lux	55155	48597	46061	45662	46213	47150	54246
Cyprus	486	505	500	437	524	425	n.a.
Denmark	16786	16136	15685	16210	16079	17116	21182
Finland	14070	13970	13041	12172	13087	13520	16273
France	107515	100873	91504	89706	92214	96033	118,809
West Germany	183180	167110	166110	160130	161610	174020	232430
Greece	4093	4772	4141	4106	4394	4293	4717
Ireland	8229	7673	7932	8437	9411	10210	10480
Italy	76788	74928	72528	72018	72965	78292	98664
Netherlands	67477	63178	50611	59307	60093	62386	67147
Norway	18649	18494	17664	18055	19140	19980	12126
Portugal	4582	4061	4122	5224	5206	5685	6049
Spain	20544	20974	21288	19858	22714	23665	22633
Sweden	30662	28389	26577	27201	29121	30172	31096
Switzerland	29265	27097	26196	33905	35756	37057	31361
Turkey	2910	4703	5890	5905	7389	8255	6244
United Kingdom	110253	102765	97081	92078	93621	100957	106785

Source: Euromonitor/Organization for Economic Co-operation and Development
(OECD)

TABLE 9. IMPORTS (FOB), IN MILLIONS OF CURRENT US DOLLARS

	1980	1981	1982	1983	1984	1985	1986
Austria	23644	20646	18813	18794	19086	20949	26229
Belgium/Lux	60310	53204	49508	47478	47431	47415	57102
Cyprus	1072	1037	1091	1090	1227	1142	1500
Denmark	18809	17063	16479	15974	16285	17887	22360
Finland	14727	13514	12753	12010	11593	12637	14609
France	120934	110843	107289	98460	96865	100565	120459
West Germany	174460	150660	141080	138650	139590	145360	175650
Greece	9650	10149	8910	8400	8624	9346	9485
Ireland	10452	9944	9094	8687	9176	10030	9634
Italy	93203	85868	80599	75236	78973	85145	95937
Netherlands	68892	59290	55947	55053	54670	57070	62759
Norway	16753	15459	15278	13704	14029	15300	15799
Portugal	8611	9121	8984	7624	7233	7142	7881
Spain	32272	31086	30542	27560	26985	27836	29121
Sweden	32860	28226	26797	25305	25697	27784	27163
Switzerland	35155	30415	28303	39299	38372	38618	34419
Turkey	7513	8567	8518	8895	10331	11230	9419
United Kingdom	106891	95594	93175	93391	99480	103240	118883

Source: IMF/Euromonitor/Organization for Economic Co-operation and Development (OECD)

TABLE 10. BALANCE OF TRADE, IN MILLIONS OF CURRENT US DOLLARS

	1980	1981	1982	1983	1984	1985	1986
Austria	−6617	−5043	−3450	−3639	−3757	−3994	−4394
Belgium/Lux	−5154	−4606	−3448	−1816	−1218	−265	−2856
Cyprus	−586	−532	−591	−654	−702	−717	n.a.
Denmark	−2023	−927	−794	236	−206	−771	−1178
Finland	−658	456	288	162	1494	882	1664
France	−13419	−9970	−15785	−8754	−4651	−4532	−1649
West Germany	8720	16460	25030	21480	22020	28660	56780
Greece	−5557	−5377	−4769	−4294	−4230	−5053	−4767
Ireland	−2222	−2270	−1162	−250	234	180	846
Italy	−16416	−10941	−8071	−3224	−6008	−6853	2727
Netherlands	−1415	3888	4663	4254	5423	5317	5604
Norway	1896	3035	2386	4351	5111	4680	−3673
Portugal	−4029	−5060	−4863	−2400	−2026	−1457	−1832
Spain	−11728	−10113	−9254	−7701	−4271	−4171	−6488
Sweden	−2198	163	−220	1896	3424	2388	2685
Switzerland	−5891	−3318	−2107	−5394	−2616	−1561	−3058
Turkey	−4603	−3864	−2628	−2990	−2942	−2975	−3175
United Kingdom	3362	7170	3906	−1312	−5859	−2284	−12100

Source: Organization for Economic Co-operation and Development (OECD)

TABLE 11. CURRENT ACCOUNT BALANCE OF PAYMENTS, IN MILLIONS OF CURRENT US DOLLARS

	1980	1981	1982	1983	1984	1985	1986e
Austria	−1725	−1464	641	246	−615	−262	−28
Belgium/Lux	−4945	−4172	−2594	−495	−55	637	3249
Cyprus	−240	−149	−156	−187	−207	−159	n.a.
Denmark	−2466	−1875	−2259	−1176	−1637	−2278	−4321
Finland	−1409	−373	−753	−936	5	−677	−808
France	−4028	−4811	−12082	−5166	−876	907	3471
West Germany	−1590	−5040	3920	4220	6770	13760	36290
Greece	−2209	−2408	−1892	−1878	−2132	−3276	−1756
Ireland	−2132	−2167	−1934	−1217	−927	−650	−450
Italy	−9745	−8644	−5706	545	−2842	−3980	5080
Netherlands	−1043	3670	4096	5049	6411	5167	5800
Norway	1098	2177	662	1986	2976	2926	−4,442
Portugal	−1064	−2065	−3250	−1004	−514	410	1135
Spain	−5173	−4989	−4245	−2746	2018	2851	4944
Sweden	−4404	−2847	−3256	−923	369	−1150	832
Switzerland	−1544	1456	3928	1209	4597	6206	7500
Turkey	−3409	−1916	−935	−1898	−1407	−1030	−1500
United Kingdom	7460	13059	6872	4730	1928	5341	−1613

Source: Euromonitor/Organization for Economic Co-operation and Development (OECD)

TABLE 12. GROSS EXTERNAL DEBT, IN BILLIONS OF CURRENT US DOLLARS

	1980	1981	1982	1983	1984	1985
Austria	12.5	13.1	11.8	10.7	10.5	13.3
Belgium	10.0	20.6	25.0	26.2	26.7	28.4
Cyprus	0.4	0.5	0.6	0.7	0.8	n.a.
Denmark	15.6	16.0	27.4	28.9	29.9	41.9
Finland	8.9	7.2	7.8	8.5	8.2	9.9
France	27.2	32.6	43.9	54.0	55.1	60.0
West Germany	70.0	106.7	113.1	105.2	96.4	131.5
Greece	7.1	8.3	9.7	10.9	12.6	16.7
Ireland*	5.7	6.0	7.4	8.0	7.9	9.7
Italy	24.6	34.8	40.5	42.5	42.4	50.1
Luxembourg	0.0	0.0	0.0	0.0	0.0	0.0
Netherlands	13.3	16.3	16.8	17.3	16.8	15.7
Norway	26.2	24.1	28.0	27.7	23.3	25.0
Portugal	8.0	11.0	13.6	14.5	15.0	16.6
Spain	23.7	27.2	28.8	29.5	29.6	28.1
Sweden	20.8	23.1	25.4	29.1	27.9	34.4
Switzerland	0.0	0.0	0.0	0.0	0.0	0.0
Turkey	15.8	19.5	20.0	20.4	22.3	25.0
United Kingdom	55.0	54.8	54.9	47.6	46.3	55.0

Source: Euromonitor
*Government debt

TABLE 13.   ENERGY CONSUMPTION BY TYPE
(Million tonnes. Data for 1984)

	Coal and lignite	Crude petroleum	Natural gas	Nuclear energy	Primary electricity*	Total primary energy (incl. others)
Austria	9.7	13.3	8.0	0.0	2.4	33.5
Belgium	10.3	17.0	7.3	7.0	0.1	41.9
Cyprus	n.a.	n.a.	n.a.	n.a.	n.a.	n.a.
Denmark	5.6	10.3	0.1	0.0	0.4	16.5
Finland	4.1	8.8	0.7	5.0	1.5	20.1
France	23.6	85.5	23.4	49.3	3.6	186.5
West Germany	84.0	107.7	40.8	22.9	1.8	257.9
Greece	5.2	10.4	0.1	0.0	0.5	16.2
Ireland	2.5	3.9	1.9	0.0	0.1	8.3
Italy	13.8	79.1	26.5	4.1	5.4	129.4
Luxembourg	0.1	1.0	0.3	0.0	0.3	3.0
Netherlands	6.7	21.4	30.8	0.9	0.3	60.2
Norway	1.0	8.2	1.2	0.0	8.2	18.7
Portugal	0.4	9.0	0.0	0.0	0.9	10.4
Spain	17.8	39.4	2.0	6.0	2.9	68.4
Sweden	2.4	14.3	0.0	14.3	5.7	36.7
Switzerland	0.6	10.8	1.3	4.9	2.1	19.7
Turkey	n.a.	n.a.	n.a.	n.a.	n.a.	n.a.
United Kingdom	45.7	87.6	43.4	14.2	0.3	192.3

Source: European Commission/Euromonitor
*Converted into oil equivalent, on the basis of 86 grams oil equivalent per kWh.

TABLE 14.   DISTRIBUTION OF ENERGY SOURCES IN PRIMARY
ENERGY CONSUMPTION
(Expressed as a percentage of total domestic consumption. Data for 1985)

	Hard coal	Lignite	Crude petroleum	Natural gas	Nuclear energy	Primary electricity	Total energy, inc. others
Austria*	5.0	20.2	59.0	5.0	0.0	5.0	100.0
Belgium	24.4	0.1	40.7	17.5	16.7	0.1	100.0
Cyprus*	5.0	0.0	90.0	0.0	0.0	3.0	100.0
Denmark	34.0	0.0	62.4	0.6	0.0	2.6	100.0
Finland*	15.0	4.0	34.0	3.0	15.0	14.0	100.0
France	12.2	0.4	45.8	12.6	26.4	1.9	100.0
West Germany	23.3	10.2	41.8	15.8	8.9	0.7	100.0
Greece	6.7	25.4	64.3	0.5	0.0	2.9	100.0
Ireland	11.8	17.7	47.0	22.6	0.0	0.7	100.0
Italy	10.4	0.2	61.1	20.5	3.2	4.2	100.0
Luxembourg	4.3	0.0	32.6	9.2	0.0	10.0	100.0
Netherlands	11.1	0.0	35.5	51.2	1.6	0.5	100.0
Norway*	10.0	0.0	60.0	20.0	0.0	10.0	100.0
Portugal	3.6	0.0	86.6	0.0	0.0	8.7	100.0
Spain	18.8	7.1	57.6	3.0	8.7	4.2	100.0
Sweden*	14.1**	—	48.0	8.0	13.2	16.7	100.0
Switzerland	2.7	1.6	65.7	7.3	15.0*	5.0*	100.0
Turkey*	40.0**	—	40.0	5.0	0.0	5.0	100.0
United Kingdom	23.8	0.0	45.6	22.6	7.4	0.2	100.0

Source: European Commission/Euromonitor
* Estimate   ** Including lignite

TABLE 15.   PETROLEUM STATISTICS 1984
(thousands of tonnes)

	Production	Imports	Refinery throughput	Refining capacity
Austria	1206	6412	7081	14300
Belgium	0	17069	23193	31200
Denmark	2314	3495	7340	8300
Finland	0	9343	10592	12000
France	2065	61112	77044	110500
West Germany	4030	48486	86565	104100
Greece	1310	11970	12693	18000
Ireland	0	0	1239	2900
Italy	2273	73177	77257	128000
Luxembourg	0	n.a.	0	0
Netherlands	3432	36560	47903	73600
Norway	34954	2252	7005	12800
Portugal	0	7375	7576	14400
Spain	2316	39669	45527	66500
Sweden	13	13756	14503	20600
Switzerland	0	4073	4080	6850
Turkey	2086	15589	17927	23050
United Kingdom	122398	28108	76921	99100

Source: European Commission

TABLE 16.   GROWTH OF INDUSTRIAL PRODUCTION
(percentage annual change, seasonally adjusted)

	1981	1982	1983	1984	1985	1986
Austria	−1.0	−1.0	0.0	6.0	4.9	1.3
Belgium	−2.6	−0.1	1.8	2.7	1.5	2.8
Cyprus	7.0	2.8	3.6	5.3	−2.5	n.a.
Denmark	0.0	2.1	3.9	10.4	4.2	3.0
Finland	2.6	1.0	2.4	4.4	3.9	0.8
France	−1.0	−1.9	1.0	0.9	2.0	1.0
West Germany	−2.0	−3.1	0.0	3.1	5.1	2.9
Greece	−1.3	5.5	−0.4	2.3	1.3	0.5*
Ireland	16.7	12.9	11.7	7.3	2.8	0.5
Italy	−1.0	−1.4	−3.2	−16.9	12.0	2.7
Luxembourg	−5.7	1.1	5.4	13.4	6.7	3.0
Netherlands	−2.0	−4.4	3.2	4.1	3.0	1.0
Norway	−1.0	0.0	9.1	8.3	−5.1	13.5
Portugal	1.0	5.0	0.0	−0.9	4.8	4.9
Spain	−0.6	−1.8	3.5	0.7	2.5	2.4
Sweden	−2.0	−1.0	4.1	7.9	1.8	0.4
Switzerland	−0.8	−4.9	−1.0	4.4	5.0	4.3
Turkey	n.a.	n.a.	n.a.	10.1	6.3	9.2
United Kingdom	−3.4	1.9	3.6	1.3	4.7	1.4

Source: Euromonitor/Organization for Economic Co- operation and Development (OECD)
* Estimate

TABLE 17. STRUCTURE OF MANUFACTURING
(proportion of total manufacturing represented by major sectors, at
1980 prices)

	Food 1970	Food 1984	Textiles/ clothing 1970	Textiles/ clothing 1984	Machinery/ transport 1970	Machinery/ transport 1984	Chemicals 1970	Chemicals 1984	Others 1970	Others 1984
Austria	15	15	12	8	21	24	5	7	47	46
Belgium	16	19	13	9	24	24	10	12	37	35
Cyprus	n.a.	n.a.	n.a.	n.a.	n.a.	n.a.	n.a.	n.a.	n.a.	n.a.
Denmark	21	22	7	6	23	23	6	8	43	40
Finland	13	11	9	7	18	22	5	6	55	54
France	16	17	10	7	29	35	10	9	36	32
West Germany	10	10	8	5	37	41	8	9	38	34
Greece	21	20	21	21	14	11	6	8	39	39
Ireland	34	32	19	10	12	18	5	15	30	25
Italy	10	11	18	18	24	25	8	8	40	38
Luxembourg	n.a.	n.a.	n.a.	n.a.	n.a.	n.a.	n.a.	n.a.	n.a.	n.a.
Netherlands	16	19	8	4	27	28	11	13	38	37
Norway	15	11	6	3	27	27	5	8	47	51
Portugal	16	16	32	28	12	11	5	7	35	37
Spain	8	13	22	15	24	20	8	8	39	44
Sweden	9	9	6	3	28	32	5	7	52	50
Switzerland	12	15	9	8	26	24	8	12	45	40
Turkey	n.a.	n.a.	n.a.	n.a.	n.a.	n.a.	n.a.	n.a.	n.a.	n.a.
United Kingdom	11	13	8	7	34	33	7	11	39	36

Source: World Bank Development Report 1987

TABLE 18. DEVELOPMENT OF CONSUMER GOODS MANUFACTURE
(base: 1980 = 100)

	1980	1983	1984	1985	1986
Austria	100.0	99.2	104.6	107.4	109.2
Belgium: Durable	100.0	101.3	99.9	101.4	106.8
Non-durable	100.0	106.6	109.3	112.1	113.4
Cyprus*	100.0	114.0	120.0	117.0	120.5
Denmark	100.0	110.0	118.0	122.0	126.0
Finland	100.0	103.0	106.0	111.0	111.0
France	100.0	101.0	101.0	102.0	101.0
West Germany	100.0	91.5	94.0	95.1	97.3
Greece	100.0	104.2	106.0	110.1	110.8
Ireland	100.0	103.6	105.5	107.2	108.4
Italy	100.0	94.2	96.3	97.5	101.1
Netherlands*	100.0	97.0	101.0	105.0	106.0
Norway	100.0	100.0	101.0	104.0	104.0
Portugal*	100.0	106.0	105.0	110.0	112.5
Spain	100.0	102.6	102.8	103.9	107.5
Sweden*	100.0	101.0	109.0	111.0	115.3
Switzerland	100.0	94.2	98.3	100.0	102.0
Turkey*	100.0	119.2	135.3	138.0	140.0
United Kingdom	100.0	98.9	101.6	103.6	105.0

Source: Organization for Economic Co-operation and Development (OECD)/Euro-
monitor
* Total manufacturing activity

169

TABLE 19. COMMERCIAL ENERGY PRODUCTION AND CONSUMPTION, 1965–1985

| | Average annual growth rate (%) | | | | Energy consumption per capita (kg of oil equivalent) | | Energy imports as a percentage of merchandise exports | |
| | Energy production | | Energy consumption | | | | | |
	1965–80	1980–85	1965–80	1980–85	1965	1985	1965	1985
Austria	0.8	−1.0	4.1	−0.7	2060	3217	10	18
Belgium	−3.9	14.5	2.9	−1.3	3402	4666	9	17
Cyprus	n.a.	n.a.	n.a.	n.a.	n.a.	n.a.	n.a.	n.a.
Denmark	2.6	63.1	2.4	0.3	2911	4001	13	19
Finland	3.9	11.4	5.4	−0.6	2233	4589	11	24
France	−0.9	9.8	3.7	−0.4	2468	3673	16	25
West Germany	−0.1	0.9	2.9	−0.1	3197	4451	8	17
Greece	10.5	12.2	8.5	2.3	615	1841	29	66
Ireland	0.0	14.2	3.9	1.8	1504	2627	14	11
Italy	1.3	1.5	3.7	0.4	1568	2606	16	30
Luxembourg	n.a.	n.a.	n.a.	n.a.	n.a.	n.a.	n.a.	n.a.
Netherlands	15.2	−0.3	4.9	−0.1	3134	5138	12	21
Norway	12.4	5.9	4.1	2.8	4650	8920	11	7
Portugal	3.5	9.3	6.3	4.3	506	1312	13	36
Spain	3.6	8.2	6.6	0.2	901	1932	31	45
Sweden	4.9	8.6	2.6	2.2	4162	6482	12	18
Switzerland	3.7	1.8	3.1	1.7	2501	3952	8	11
Turkey	n.a.	n.a.	n.a.	n.a.	n.a.	n.a.	n.a.	n.a.
United Kingdom	3.6	2.6	0.8	0.0	3481	3603	13	14

Source: World Bank Development Report 1987

TABLE 20. OUTPUT OF SELECTED AGRICULTURAL PRODUCE, 1985 (thousands of tonnes)

	Wheat	Potatoes	Beef/veal	Pork/bacon	Milk
Austria	1563	1042	225	463	3797
Belgium	1150	1532	316	706	3037*
Cyprus	18**	180**	4**	22**	53**
Denmark	1996	1073	252	1132	5099
Finland	478	745	123	169	3150
France	29735	6200**	4656	18468	2465*
West Germany	25914	7905**	1567**	3232	25674
Greece**	2646	980	83	151	700
Ireland	660	800	464	146	5809
Italy	8516	2565	1215	1190	11000
Luxembourg	20	15	14	7	297
Netherlands	895	6673**	520**	1320**	13000
Norway**	145	470	76	84	2020
Portugal	1450	1171	89	179	740
Spain	5326	5949**	382	1160	6500
Sweden	1654	1307**	141	331	3647
Switzerland	547	848	170	277	3700
Turkey	17000	3600	245**	0	3600**
United Kingdom	11954	5473	1115	945	6896*

Source: National statistics/Euromonitor
* Million litres   ** 1984

TABLE 21.   AGRICULTURE AND FERTILIZER CONSUMPTION, 1970–1985

	Agricultural value added (millions of 1980 dollars) 1970	1985	Fertilizer consumption (hundred gms of plant nutrient per hectare of arable land) 1970	1984	Average index of per capita food production (1979–81 = 100) 1983–1985
Austria	2,939	3,565	2,517	2,522	108
Belgium	2,370	3,220	5,686	5,382	98
Cyprus	n.a.	n.a.	n.a.	n.a.	n.a.
Denmark	2,490	4,020	2,254	2,660	118
Finland	4,096	4,265	1,931	2,220	114
France	24,070	30,219	2,424	3,115	107
West Germany	14,859	19,040	4,208	4,211	110
Greece	4,929	6,164	858	1,611	104
Ireland	n.a.	n.a.	3,573	6,973	108
Italy	22,099	25,215	962	1,684	103
Luxembourg	n.a.	n.a.	n.a.	n.a.	n.a.
Netherlands	3,949	8,492	7,165	7,879	107
Norway	2,035	2,455	2,471	2,970	109
Portugal	n.a.	2,380	411	634	100
Spain	10,929	15,999	595	710	104
Sweden	4,067	4,477	1,639	1,603	108
Switzerland	n.a.	n.a.	3,842	4,296	108
Turkey	n.a.	n.a.	n.a.	n.a.	n.a.
United Kingdom	7,907	11,476	2,521	3,746	109

Source: World Bank Development Report 1987

TABLE 22.   SHARE PRICE MOVEMENTS
Development of national stock exchange indices, in major European equity centres
(base: 1980 = 100)

	1980	1981	1982	1983	1984	1985	1986
Austria	100	89	79	86	89	170	212
Belgium	100	81	96	120	154	171	246
Denmark	100	167	213	372	401	416	410
Finland	100	103	138	210	295	253	389
France	100	88	75	101	136	159	238
West Germany	100	100	99	134	150	200	270
Ireland	100	104	85	106	140	149	240
Italy	100	152	123	153	172	287	667*
Luxembourg	100	87	78	88	102	152	230
Netherlands	100	106	107	155	197	255	335
Norway	100	98	92	142	202	267	282
Spain	100	127	117	118	162	204	416*
Sweden	100	149	186	360	394	367	599
Switzerland	100	91	90	116	132	172	209
United Kingdom	100	113	130	165	196	242	312

Source: Euromonitor
* [sic]

TABLE 23. BANK DISCOUNT RATES
(%)

	1980	1981	1982	1983	1984	1985	1986
Austria	6.75	6.75	4.75	3.75	4.50	4.00	4.00
Belgium	12.00	15.00	11.50	10.00	11.00	9.75	8.00
Cyprus	6.00	6.00	6.00	6.00	6.00	6.00	6.00
Denmark	11.00	11.00	10.00	7.00	7.00	7.00	7.00
Finland	9.25	9.25	8.50	9.50	15.07	9.00	7.00
France	9.50	9.50	9.50	9.50	9.50	9.50	9.50
West Germany	7.50	7.50	5.00	4.00	4.50	4.00	3.50
Greece	20.50	20.50	20.50	20.50	20.50	20.50	20.50
Ireland	14.00	16.50	14.00	12.25	14.00	10.25	13.25
Italy	16.50	19.00	18.00	17.00	16.50	15.00	12.00
Luxembourg*	9.25	9.63	10.00	9.38	9.25	8.75	7.75
Netherlands	8.00	9.00	5.00	5.00	5.00	5.00	4.50
Norway	9.00	9.00	9.00	8.00	8.00	8.00	8.00
Portugal	18.00	18.00	18.75	23.17	25.00	23.50	16.75
Spain	8.00		8.00	8.00	8.00	8.00	8.00
Sweden	10.00	11.00	10.00	8.50	9.50	10.50	7.50
Switzerland	3.00	6.00	4.50	4.00	4.00	4.00	4.00
Turkey	26.00	31.50	31.50	48.50	52.00	58.00	n.a.
United Kingdom	14.08	10.56	8.82	6.46	6.37	8.87	8.50

Source: Euromonitor
* Deposit rate

TABLE 24. AREA AND POPULATION DENSITY

	Area (sq. km)	Population density per sq. km (1986)	Average annual population growth 1973–1985
Austria	83853	90	0.0
Belgium	30519	287	0.1
Cyprus	9251*	72	0.7
Denmark	43080	119	0.1
Finland	338130	14	0.4
France	543965	101	0.5
West Germany	249535	102	−0.1
Greece	131957	75	1.0
Ireland	70283	51	1.2
Italy	301277	190	0.3
Luxembourg	2586	142	0.3
Netherlands	41160	350	0.6
Norway	323895	13	0.4
Portugal	92072	111	1.0
Spain	504782	76	0.9
Sweden	448964	19	0.2
Switzerland	41293	154	0.1
Turkey	779452	38	2.2
United Kingdom	244103	230	0.0

Source: World Bank/National statistics
* Including 4163 km of territory occupied by Turkey

TABLE 25.   CURRENT AND PROJECTED POPULATION STRUCTURE,
BY AGE GROUP

	1985 (Latest statistical information)			1990		
	0–14	**15–64**	**65+**	**0–14**	**15–64**	**65+**
Austria	13.6	72.0	14.4	17.6	67.3	15.1
Belgium	19.4	66.6	14.0	18.9	66.3	14.8
Cyprus	25.0	64.2	10.8	25.0	65.0	10.0
Denmark	19.0	66.1	14.9	16.8	67.6	15.6
Finland	19.5	68.1	12.4	19.0	69.0	12.0
France	21.7	65.2	13.1	21.1	65.4	13.5
West Germany	15.9	69.5	14.6	15.3	70.1	14.6
Greece	21.5	65.2	13.3	22.7	64.6	12.7
Ireland	30.0	65.2	10.6	28.0	60.0	12.0
Italy	21.1	59.2	13.6	18.0	67.6	14.4
Luxembourg	18.0	68.6	13.4	18.2	69.1	12.7
Netherlands	20.4	76.2	11.9	18.9	68.4	12.7
Norway	20.7	68.7	10.6	20.0	69.0	11.0
Portugal	23.7	64.3	12.0	23.7	65.2	11.1
Spain	24.2	64.1	11.7	20.8	34.0	13.2
Sweden	18.2	64.6	17.2	18.0	68.0	14.0
Switzerland	18.2	68.0	13.8	18.0	68.0	14.0
Turkey	38.6	56.8	4.6	39.0	57.0	4.0
United Kingdom	19.2	66.0	14.8	19.2	64.9	15.9

Source: Euromonitor

TABLE 26.   PROJECTED FERTILITY AND LIFE EXPECTANCY,
1970 AND 1984

	Life expectancy (years)		Total fertility*	
	1970	**1984**	**1970**	**1984**
Austria	70	73	2.3	1.6
Belgium	71	75	2.3	1.6
Cyprus	71	75	2.6	2.4
Denmark	73	75	2.2	1.4
Finland	70	75	1.9	1.7
France	72	77	2.5	1.9
West Germany	70	75	2.1	1.4
Greece	72	75	2.4	2.1
Ireland	71	73	3.9	2.7
Italy	72	77	2.4	1.6
Luxembourg	70	74	1.9	1.5
Netherlands	74	77	2.5	1.5
Norway	74	77	2.6	1.7
Portugal	67	74	2.9	2.0
Spain	72	77	2.9	2.1
Sweden	74	77	2.1	1.6
Switzerland	73	77	2.1	1.5
Turkey	56	64	5.3	3.9
United Kingdom	72	74	2.4	1.8

Source: World Bank, based on projections.
*The number of children expected to be born to an average woman who is born
during the year in question

TABLE 27. DEVELOPMENT OF THE LABOUR FORCE
(percentage annual increase, seasonally adjusted

	1985 total ('000)	1984	1985	1986	1987e	1988 (projection)
Austria	3355	0.6	−0.2	0.7	0.5	0.5
Belgium	4202	0.0	−0.3	−0.1	0.25	0.25
Denmark	2784	1.0	1.7	0.7	0.75	0.75
Finland	2556	0.7	0.8	0.3	0.25	0.25
France	23864	0.6	0.2	0.3	0.75	0.75
West Germany	27838	0.1	0.8	0.6	0.5	0.5
Greece	3892	0.7	0.6	−0.3	0.25	0.25
Ireland	1299	0.4	−1.1	−0.9	−0.5	−0.25
Italy	23274	0.2	0.8	1.6	1.0	0.75
Luxembourg	163	0.7	1.4	1.3	1.5	1.5
Netherlands	5322	0.0	−0.2	0.3	0.0	0.0
Norway	2064	0.3	1.6	2.3	1.75	0.5
Portugal	4448	−1.1	−0.5	0.2	0.5	0.5
Spain	13542	0.6	0.8	1.8	1.5	1.0
Sweden	4400	0.3	0.9	0.7	0.5	0.5
Switzerland	3195	0.1	0.6	0.8	1.25	0.75
Turkey	18769	1.3	1.4	1.3	1.25	1.25
United Kingdom	27644	1.6	1.6	0.7	0.5	0.5

Source: Organization for Economic Co-operation and Development (OECD)

TABLE 28. UNEMPLOYMENT
(registered unemployed, expressed as a proportion of the registered workforce)

	1980	1981	1982	1983	1984	1985	1986
Austria	1.7	2.4	3.7	4.5	4.5	4.8	5.0
Belgium	9.2	9.8	11.0	12.1	12.2	12.1	11.8
Cyprus	2.1	1.7	2.8	3.3	3.3	3.5	4.0
Denmark	6.9	9.2	9.8	10.4	10.0	10.0	8.0
Finland	4.8	5.3	6.3	6.1	6.2	6.3	6.9
France	6.2	7.7	8.6	8.9	10.0	10.2	10.3
West Germany	4.3	5.5	7.7	9.1	9.1	9.3	9.0
Greece	2.4	4.7	5.8	7.4	8.0	8.4	9.3
Ireland	5.9	6.6	7.8	15.2	16.5	17.8	18.0
Italy	7.4	8.4	9.1	9.3	10.4	10.8	11.0
Luxembourg	0.7	1.1	1.3	1.6	1.7	1.6	1.4
Netherlands	4.7	9.0	12.6	15.2	15.3	14.2	13.0
Norway	1.2	1.7	2.5	3.3	3.3	2.5	2.0
Portugal	7.5	7.7	7.4	8.2	11.0	10.9	10.9
Spain	7.8	11.8	16.3	17.7	20.6	21.9	21.5
Sweden	1.4	1.9	2.5	3.5	3.1	3.0	3.1
Switzerland	0.2	0.2	0.4	0.9	1.1	1.0	0.8
Turkey	7.4	11.3	11.8	14.0	16.5	16.7	19.0
United Kingdom	7.4	9.4	10.9	11.9	12.4	12.9	13.0

Source: National statistics/Euromonitor

TABLE 29. HEALTH PERSONNEL AND EQUIPMENT
(data for 1982/83)

	Hospital beds	Hospital beds per 10,000 inhabitants	Doctors	Doctors per 10,000 inhabitants	Pharmacists	Pharmacists per 10,000 inhabitants	Dentists	Dentists per 10,000 inhabitants
Austria	84000	111.6	12425	16.5	—	—	1958	2.6
Belgium	92100	93.0	26593	27.0	10177	10.3	5132	5.2
Cyprus	3500	53.8	601	9.4	—	—	178	2.7
Denmark	39600	77.0	12120	23.7	340	0.7	5001	9.8
Finland	74400	154.7	9583	19.8	—	—	4162	8.6
France	595900	109.0	114951	21.0	21811	4.0	33048	6.0
West Germany	682700	111.0	149912	24.4	30006	4.9	34187	5.6
Greece	57400	58.0	27607	28.1	5384	5.5	8222	8.4
Ireland	31900	91.0	5200	14.8	1120	3.2	1109	3.2
Italy	515200	91.0	202487	35.8	46383	8.2	14283	2.5
Luxembourg	4700	128.0	627	17.1	246	6.7	147	4.0
Netherlands	170300	119.0	29951	20.3	1728	1.2	6586	4.6
Norway	67800	164.6	8998	21.9	—	—	3410	8.3
Portugal	58600	59.6	19939	20.1	—	—	987	9.9
Spain	201500	53.6	102411	27.0	—	—	4552	1.2
Sweden	134200	161.1	17993	21.6	—	—	9079	11.0
Switzerland	76300	119.2	10368	16.0	—	—	3912	6.1
Turkey	97800	21.5	28411	6.1	—	—	6790	1.4
United Kingdom	439800	78.0	81122	14.4	—	—	16325	2.9

Source: European Commission/World Bank

175

TABLE 30. PUPILS IN PRIMARY AND SECONDARY EDUCATION
(Thousands. Figures for 1982/83)

	Total	Pre-school	Primary	Secondary
Austria	1236.8	163.7	367.7	705.4
Belgium	2049.9	389.8	812.1	848.1
Cyprus	107.2	12.5	46.2	48.5
Denmark	989.4	61.5	431.9	495.9
Finland	885.6	86.8	366.0	432.8
France	12159.6	2407.9	4478.1	5273.7
West Germany	10661.1	1586.8	2529.8	6544.5
Greece	1726.7	153.6	890.2	376.5
Ireland	891.7	143.0	431.8	316.9
Italy	11281.6	1757.4	4204.3	5319.9
Luxembourg	55.9	7.6	24.0	24.3
Netherlands	3143.7	398.8	1297.2	1447.7
Norway	835.1	82.9	383.6	368.6
Portugal	1430.1	72.3	945.2	412.6
Spain	8871.2	1197.9	3633.7	4039.6
Sweden	1498.2	232.9	658.1	607.2
Switzerland	986.2	120.1	415.5	450.6
Turkey	5865.4	5.1	5859.7	2393.5
United Kingdom	10229.0	323.0	4522.0	5384.0

Source: European Commission

TABLE 31. TRANSPORT STATISTICS

	Year	Paved roads (km)	Motorways (km)	Railways (km)
Austria	1984	10256	1137	6321
Belgium	1985	130311	1488	3741
Cyprus	1985	4000	0	0
Denmark	1984	69827	518	2931
Finland	1985	37817	200	6069
France	1986	1050000	5000	38000
West Germany	1985	500000	8080	32000
Greece	1986	11000	0	2650
Ireland	1986	80500	300	1968
Italy	1985	298964	1250	20065
Luxembourg	1985	5157	0	270
Netherlands	1984	53848	1819	2852
Norway	1986	53987	500	4242
Portugal	1986	22545	300	3614
Spain	1985	155543	1963	13572
Sweden	1984	87136	1000	11707
Switzerland	1984	66544	1000	5900
Turkey	1983	63201	n.a.	9810
United Kingdom	1986	370000	2897	18400

Source: National statistics/Euromonitor

TABLE 32.   TV AND RADIO RECEIVERS, 1987
(estimates based on national statistics)

	TV sets (million)	TVs per '000 inhabitants (1983)	Radio receivers (million)	Radios per '000 inhabitants (1983)
Austria	2.5	311	2.5	530
Belgium	3.4	303	4.9	468
Cyprus	0.2	369	0.4	623
Denmark	1.9	432	2.1	392
Finland	2.1	369	4.0	987
France	23.2	375	48.1	860
West Germany	25.0	360	27.0	401
Greece	3.0	173	3.5	406
Ireland	0.9	293	1.8	456
Italy	18.7	243	18.0	250
Luxembourg	0.2	308	0.3	537
Netherlands	6.4	450	12.0	793
Norway	1.3	315	3.1	377
Portugal	1.7	155	2.4	166
Spain	11.0	258	11.5	290
Sweden	3.2	387	8.4	858
Switzerland	2.2	376	2.8	381
Turkey	7.0	124	6.5	96
United Kingdom	23.0	457	54.0	995

Source: Euromonitor

INDEX

(Figures and Tables in **Bold**)